LAWMEN AND ROBBERS

LAWMEN AND ROBBERS

by

Carl W. Breihan

The CAXTON PRINTERS, Ltd.
Caldwell, Idaho 83605
1986

Library of Congress Cataloging-in-Publication Data

Breihan, Carl W., 1915-
   Lawmen and robbers.

   Bibliography: p.
   1. Peace officers — West (U.S.) — Biography.
2. Outlaws — West (U.S.) — Biography. 3. Frontier and
pioneer life — West (U.S.) 4. West (U.S.) — History.
5. West (U.S.) — Biography. I. Title.
F596.B84 1986   978'.02'0922 [B]   85-25447
ISBN 0-87004-318-8

Lithographed and bound in the United States of America by
The CAXTON PRINTERS, Ltd.
Caldwell, Idaho 83605
143751

TO THE CULBERTSONS:
FRANK, PEARL, ROBERT,
JAN, FRANCIS, and DANIEL FRANCIS,
JUDY, JIM and JILL

Contents

Illustrations

Acknowledgments

WITHOUT THE DEDICATED assistance of hundreds of wonderful people and many, many historical societies and chambers of commerce, such a work as this would never become a reality. My thanks and humble appreciation to those whose names follow; should I omit someone, believe me, it is unintentional:

Jay Doolin Meek, son of Bill Doolin; Sam Ream, historian at Dover, Ohio; Milt Hinkle, famous rodeo rider and researcher of the Old West; Barney Hubbs, president, West of the Pecos Museum, Pecos, Texas; Buffalo Vernon Averill, who, as a lad, suffered untold agonies on the Sweetwater; Wayne Montgomery, whose own experiences and those of his grandfather are fantastic exploits; Kerry Ross Boren, meticulous researcher, Salt Lake City, Utah; Mary P. Young, Clayton, New Mexico; E. M. Dickey; Elmer Sparks, Canadian, Texas; Bill Selman, grandson of John Selman; Bill Morrison, expert on Pancho Villa, El Paso, Texas; Bob Mullin, expert historian of the southwest, South Laguna, California; John Hughes, famous Texas Ranger, whom I knew well, and Fr. Stanley.

Many other sources furnished expert assistance: Uvalde, Texas, Chamber of Commerce; Clayton, New Mexico, Chamber of Commerce; and others too numerous to mention. Hundreds of contemporary newspapers were read and researched to authenticate this material, as well as the records of penal intitutions searched for information.

It is hoped that this compilation of Western Americana will prove interesting to you, the reader, My thanks.

Carl W. Breihan
St. Louis, Missouri

Introduction

IN THIS TEXT, author Breihan presents an interesting and informative account of characters about whom too much has not been written, with the exception perhaps of "Butch" Cassidy and Bill Doolin.

Some of these subjects were new to me, even though I have been a student of Western Americana for many years. I was impressed with his account of the last days of Laura Bullion, a little known fact of this sweetheart of Ben Kilpatrick. Few people realized that she had been killed in Argentina prior to the death of Ben, and this information is an interesting facet in the history of the Hole-in-the-Wall bunch.

Author Breihan has done his usual excellent job of tracing the movements of these men through that post-Civil War era when men were men and guns spoke loud and often. His story of Buffalo Vernon Averill was new to me, and certainly a thrilling addition to this book.

Carl W. Breihan's ability to gather a fascinating display of new and sometimes rare photos has always amazed me, and his personal contact with the sons of Bill Doolin and the James brothers has always been a most intriguing aspect of his excellent research work. Contacts with the daughter of Burton Mossman and with Buffalo Vernon lends a touch of authenticity to this work.

While I cannot comment on all the characters in this work, I am sure the reader will be as pleased with the new data and photos as I was. It is a refreshing thought to learn of new subjects every now and then.

Author Breihan has already established himself as an authority of the James-Younger boys histories, a fact admitted by the late Homer Croy, who was never one to admit that anyone could know more about the subject than he. He admitted that Breihan was the first to document the fact that Frank James had killed the bookkeeper at the Northfield, Minnesota, bank raid, and not Jesse, as all believed. Croy even wrote an introduction to Breihan's very first book dealing with the life of Jesse James. He said this in one section of this introduction: "Carl W. Breihan has fetched to light an immense amount of new material. It was unknown to me and I have been sleeping with Jesse James for years. Where he got all this new information is beyond me."

Breihan's areas of interest are not limited to the James-Youngers however, for his knowledge of Quantrill, Polk Wells, Bill Hickman, and Sam Hildebrand is on a par with his many other accomplishments. His most notable accomplishment, aside from his interesting and easy style, is his apparent careful research, thorough documentation, and un-opinionated and straight-forward presentation.

All of these things make his books and other writings not only interesting reading, but valuable pieces of recorded history. He is also to be commended for his graceful acceptance of criticism, correcting noted errors in updated reissues on his works with no excuses or comment.

Kerry Ross Boren
Historian and Author
Vernal, Utah

LAWMEN AND ROBBERS

Chapter One

Black Bart, Stagecoach Robber

SPARKS OF static electricity snapped loudly in the elegantly furnished office of the San Francisco headquarters of the Wells Fargo Company as Detective James Hume paced nervously over the heavy carpet.

Seated at a carved mahogany desk, his face cupped in his hands, was the comptroller of the Wells Fargo Company. He said nothing, apparently waiting for Hume to make a statement. It was not long in coming.

"Dammit," exploded the fiery Chief of Detectives of the firm, "why must we be plagued with this stage robber? Is there no end to it? If I was not reasonably sure that Jesse James was back in Missouri, I'd swear he was the cause of all our present trouble."

Who was this daring stage robber who boldly held up stages in broad daylight and all alone? Who was this man who wore a long linen duster and a flour sack for a mask, and who robbed numerous stages without firing a shot? These were the questions to which Detective James Hume sought to find the answers.

This outlaw was a humorous cuss with it all. Although he cowed driver and passengers with a double-barreled shotgun, he also took time to leave bits of poetry in his wake . . .

Wells Fargo Bank History Room

Dapper Black Bart, whose real name was Charles E. Boles, drove lawmen wild with his smooth work as a road agent in California. He wore two hats and went unidentified for years to become a legend.

Wells Fargo Bank History Room

Stagecoaches such as this fine Concord were fair game for Black Bart. Coaches running to the mines of the Mother Lode, often hauling gold dust and/or coin, were especially lucrative.

poetry which was written in a disguised manner, but appeared that of an educated man.

The story of Charles E. Boles, alias "Black Bart," reads like so much fiction, and in his case, the term that "truth is stranger that fiction" certainly can be applied. He used other names during his lifetime also, among which were Charles E. Boulton and Charles E. Bolton.

Charles E. Boles was born in New York State in 1835, and made his way west at an early age. However, three years of hard work in the California gold mines, and gaining nothing, convinced Boles to return east. He settled in Illinois for awhile, and there met a young girl whom he later married and by whom he had three daughters.

Boles was no slacker. When the Civil War broke out, he volunteered in the Illinois Volunteer Infantry and was assigned to Company B as a first lieutenant. He served with distinc-tion throughout the entire war, gaining the rank of captain. After his discharge from the army in 1865, Boles returned to his family in Illinois, remaining there for about a year. The wanderlust again tugging at his heels, Boles moved his family to Oregon, but found this area not to his liking, so he set out for Montana, leaving his family behind. It must be said that he kept in touch with his wife and children for about two years; then all communication ceased abruptly. Word finally reached Mrs. Boles that her husband and several friends had been killed by Indians in Montana. With a heavy heart, she and her children joined her parents in Missouri.

But the facts of Boles' death were greatly exaggerated. In 1874, he was seen at the race tracks in San Antonio, apparently well-to-do, sporting a derby hat, a fine suit, and swinging an elegant cane. Boles was indeed a pure gentleman. He never carried a weapon, talked

2

Henry Wells (left) and William Fargo lost fortunes to Black Bart, put a price on his head, and were driven to distraction trying to find the slippery outlaw. Often their Wells Fargo agents failed.

little, but when he did, he used excellent English. His dress was immaculate, and he paid special attention to such details as elegant ties and diamond stick pins, and always displaying the best of manners to male or female. He never smoked, drank, gambled or cursed. Moreover, he loved good jokes, even played on himself.

Boles reached California in 1875, having informed his friends in Texas that he was going to set up a "business" there. In San Francisco, he became a resident of a plush hotel, setting himself up under the alias of Charles E. Bolton, a wealthy mine owner. It was noted by many that he left the city at intervals to "inspect" his mines in upper California and Nevada. A fact that everyone missed was that whenever Bolton returned from his mining inspection tours, Wells Fargo Company was losing money.

It all began when Johnny Shine, expertly guiding the big team down a familiar but dangerous stage route on July 26, 1875, was suddenly confronted by a white-shrouded figure with a double-barreled shotgun pointed at his head.

"Throw down the strong box and the mail bag!" ordered the holdup man. "Be quick about it!"

As Shine struggled to control his frightened team, he managed to kick the money box off the stage and to throw down the mail pouch. This was Black Bart's first stage robbery — the run from Sonora to Milton.

Other robberies occurred. On December 28, 1875, the stage from San Juan to Marysville was robbed, the holdup man ordering driver Mike Hogan to leave the area posthaste. On June 2, 1876, A. C. Adams was accosted by the shrouded figure as he drove his stage from Roseburg to Yreka.

"He's like a ghost," Adams told the au-

3

thorities. "All you can see is his eyes behind the slits in the flour sack and the yawning barrels of that damned shotgun."

The robber was always courteous and soft-spoken, assuring the driver no harm would befall him if he obeyed instructions. As soon as the strong box would hit the ground, the bandit would break off the lock with a heavy bar, rifle it and the mail bags; then slither into the brush and disappear.

On August 3, 1877, as the Point Arena-Duncan Mills stage bounced along the brush-lined trail, a lone bandit leaped from the bushes, a shotgun covering the driver. A command of "Hands Up!" caused the driver to slam on his brakes and instantly obey.

"Turn your back and don't move until you are told."

The bandit then broke open the strong box, rifled the mail bags, and disappeared into the brush. As soon as the coast was clear the driver sent his horses at breakneck speed into Duncan Mills, the stage careening wildly into the booming lumber town.

Racing to the railroad office, the driver sent a graphic account of the robbery to the Wells Fargo office in San Francisco. While waiting the arrival of Detective Hume, a posse went to the scene of the holdup, and began a search. On a waybill of the express company, the robber had scrawled the following lines:

Here I lay me down to sleep
to wait the coming morrow
perhaps success, perhaps defeat
and everlasting sorrow,
Let come what may, I'll try it on,
my condition can't be worse.
And if there's money in that box,
'tis munny in my purse
Black Bart, PO-8

Six-horse hitches like this one plied the foothills and wilderness trails of Placer County and the Mother Lode. Black Bart might bring one to a halt most anywhere, anytime . . .

On July 25, 1878, the stage plying between Quincy and Oroville was held up and robbed by the mysterious bandit; again the money box was rifled and the mail bag slit open and pilfered. On July 30th the lone bandit stopped the stage of Dan Barry as he drove from Laporte to Butte. As in all previous cases, the same method of operation was used, and when the posse arrived, no trace of the daring fellow could be found.

Not content with robbing the stage on October 2, 1878, on the Cahto-Ukiah line, the robber struck the next day and held up the stage on Cavelo-Potter-Ukiah line. Today, there is a large rock between Ukiah and Willits, California, which is called "Black Bart Rock." He used to hide behind this rock and hold up the stages in that area. Black Bart kept a room at the Commercial Hotel in Ukiah, and when this building was torn down in the 1930s, a pencil drawing signed Black Bart on the back side was found therein.

When Detective Hume ordered armed guards to ride, hidden, in a stage on any certain line, Black Bart seemed to know about it almost as soon as the order was given, and usually struck another unguarded stage in another district. Hume's first break came when a rancher informed him that a stranger, dressed in miner's garb, had stopped at his place for food. He described the man as average height, lean body and wide shoulders, weight about one hundred fifty pounds, his eyes a light grey and deep set, heavy eyebrows, black hair sprinkled with gray, and a heavy mustache and imperial. Bart's miner's guise permitted him to roam the terrain around each holdup point until he knew the area to perfection. When a posse arrived, he had either holed up in a cave or some hollow log, or had outdistanced them on foot over ground too rough for horses. Black Bart always carried a good change of clothing in a blanket roll, enabling him to dress the part of a successful city man when he felt inclined to do so.

With the approach of fall, Bolton returned to his San Francisco address at the Webb House. He took his meals at a local restaurant, which was also patronized by police officers and newspaper reporters. As Black Bart was a top subject, he avidly absorbed all the latest news as to what was being done in regard to the elusive bandit. He smiled as he thought of how he had taken the name "Black Bart" from a newspaper fiction story, and how he had decided to use a white disguise as an amusing touch to the name.

On June 21, 1879, Black Bart began his mining inspection tour by robbing the stage operated by Dave Quadlin on the line running between Laporte and Oroville, securing all available loot and doing his usual disappearing act. On October 25, another stage was robbed on the Roseburg-Redding line, and to add insult to injury, two days later he robbed the stage on the Alturas-Redding stage line. This remarkable little man then walked fifty miles before pausing, again eluding his would-be

Black Bart had a weakness for Wells Fargo strong boxes which kept him "in business" and able to live in high style.
Wells Fargo Bank History Room

The Colt, Wells Fargo pocket pistol, was designed for express guards, police and Wells Fargo agents. It was introduced in 1849, year of the California gold rush.
Wells Fargo Bank History Room

James Hume, chief of detectives for Wells Fargo, dogged Black Bart all over California and investigated the many holdups. The road agent became a personal project for Hume, who finally brought him in.

captors. In November, he was back at the Webb House.

On July 22, 1880, as driver M. K. McLennan neared his stage to Henry Station, on the Point Arena-Duncan Mills run, the Jack-in-the-Box bandit appeared suddenly upon the scene. The stage was halted as usual by a lone, hooded figure standing in the middle of the road. The driver was doubly careful this time, for he could see several rifle barrels protruding from the bushes, as well as men's hats. It was later discovered that Bart's "confederates" had been a half dozen black painted broom handles and old hats.

In September, Black Bart continued his vocation by robbing the stage of driver Charles Cramer as it rolled leisurely along the dusty road on the Weaverville-Redding line. He then worked his way into Tehama County and disappeared. On September 16, he again hit the headlines and Detective Hume "hit the ceiling" when the stage on the Roseburg-Yreka line was robbed as driver Nort Eddings traveled south. Apparently pickings must have been good, for Black Bart remained in that area until January 1881, during which time

he robbed the Redding-Roseburg stage operated by Joe Mason on November 20, 1880.

Back in San Francisco, the bold bandit lived a life of leisure and contentment. Evidently his hauls during the year 1880 had been great, for he did not hit the trail again until the latter part of the following year.

On August 31, 1881, the bandit appeared back in the lucrative area where he had spent the previous winter. His first "mine" came rolling down the trail of the Roseburg-Yreka stage line, driver John Lulloway taking his time and humming a jolly tune. In short order, he was robbed of all the valuables the stage carried, and was ordered to "get" down the road, which he did post haste. On October 8, the Yreka-Redding stage operated by Horace Williams was intercepted as it neared Bass Station on the stage line. Three days later, the shrouded robber struck again, holding up the Lakeview-Redding stage driven by Louis Brewster, as his team trudged up the grade of Round Mountain. No driver argued with the now-familiar hooded bandit and did as instructed. A large posse was formed, but without results. By the time the officers had become organized, Black Bart was in Butte County, where all trace of him vanished.

On December 15, 1881, the stage of driver George Sharpe was stopped and robbed on the Downieville-Marysville route. Back on the job again on the twenty-seventh, the bold Bart secured a good haul from the stage on the North San Juan-Smartsville line, after which he departed from Yuba County. To start off the year 1882 in proper manner, Bolton robbed the stage of the Ukiah-Cloverdale line on January 26. As usual, driver Harry Forse could give no more information about the bandit than was already known. The usual excited posse appeared on the scene, to no avail. Black Bart was tracked as far as Kelseyville, and there the trail ended.

On June 14, as the stage of Thomas B. Forse rolled along the trail near Little Lake, it was held up and robbed by the lone bandit. On July 13, Black Bart met his first resistance when he stopped the stage of George Helms, plying between Laporte and Oroville. The stage was carrying a large sum of money and

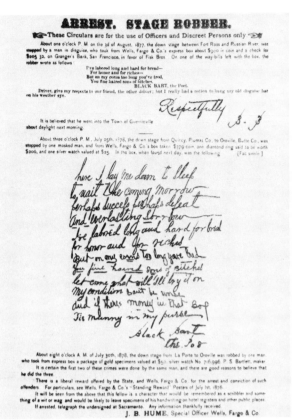

Circulars, handbills and posters such as this were published in hope of tracking the identity of the mysterious road agent. Bart taunted his adversaries with doggerel and free-verse poetry, often found in the empty strong boxes.

Samples of Bart's writings were circulated far and wide, also offers of $1,000 reward for his capture.

Black Bart carried this shotgun in his holdups, but claimed it was always empty. He never killed nor wounded anyone . . .

This early layout of sketches showed how the legendary Black Bart operated. Stories of how the road agent outwitted lawmen persist to this day.

to protect it, the company had installed a shotgun messenger to ride with Helms. When the bandit leaped into the road and ordered the stage driver to halt, guard George W. Hackett sent a load of buckshot winging at the highwayman. Black Bart lost all interest in the strong box, and fled into the brush as fast as he could. The posse later found a derby hat at the scene, in which several holes made by the .00 buckshot were discovered.

Undaunted by his sad experience with the buckshot, Black Bart again appeared upon the scene when he held up and robbed the stage of Horace Williams on September 17, about twelve miles from Yreka. The holdup man requested the driver to convey his respects to Detective Hume, chief special agent of the Wells Fargo Company.

On November 24, 1882, Black Bart struck the stage line some six miles out of Cloverdale on the Lakeport-Cloverdale line. The driver, Ed Crawford, raced his team into town and a posse took the trail, which led toward Lower Lake. But again, this vigorous walker was too much for the posse.

Black Bart opened his 1883 season by robbing the stage of driver Connibeck on the Lakeport-Cloverdale line on April 12. He forced the driver to unhitch his horses and to drive them some distance behind the stage. Black Bart then rifled the strong box, took to the brush and again made good his escape.

On June 23 Black Bart was in Amador County, where he held up the stage of Clint Radcliffe on the Jackson-Ione City line. His haul packed in his duster, he went his merry way, and from a safe distance watched through his binoculars as the disgruntled lawmen chased themselves around the scene of the holdup. Bart also used his binoculars to spot hidden guards in stages that had been "set up" for him.

Anxious to lay in a goodly supply of gold for the winter, Black Bart next stopped the stage of R. McConnell as it rambled over the Sonora-Milton line on November 3, 1883. As the stage topped a grade in the trail, Black Bart appeared suddenly and ordered the driver to halt, then unhitch his animals and place them some distance out-of-sight over the rise.

What the bandit did not know was that a young lad about eighteen years old had been hunting with a .22 calibre rifle, and that the driver was motioning the lad to come toward him. They both then edged toward the crest of the hill, from which vantage point the boy fired at the robber. Black Bart jumped as if hit, then drove for the brush.

Before leaving the scene, and realizing that speed now was the most important thing before him, Black Bart secreted his booty in a hollow stump and made tracks out of the district. Behind a huge boulder, where the bandit had waited for the stage to appear, the posse found a pair of field glasses, a heavy pry-bar, several white flour sacks, a derby hat, and a blood-stained handkerchief with the laundry mark FXO-7 on it. The evidence was placed in the hands of Detective Hume, who then called in his assistants, Harry N. Morse and John N. Thacker, for a consultation.

It was agreed by the manhunters that the laundry mark probably would not have been used in any small towns in the area, so it was decided to check the San Francisco area first, even though it seemed like a "wild goose chase."

One by one the laundries in the Bay Area were contacted. Detective Morse had about run out of places, his men had visited almost a hundred laundries without results, when Morse reached a tobacco shop run by T. C. Ware on Bush Street, who also acted as agent for the California Laundry on Stevenson Street. When shown the laundry mark, he had no difficulty in tracing it to a customer named Charles E. Bolton.

"Sure, I know Mr. Bolton; he's a mining man, lives at the Webb House, and goes to California and Nevada each summer to inspect his mines."

Morse left the tobacco shop and rushed to the police station, persuaded Captain Stone to send some officers to check the Webb House, then raced back to the tobacco shop in case Bolton put in an appearance there. He was again in conversation with Mr. Ware when the storekeeper looked out the window and exclaimed, "You're lucky you came back; there he is now."

Charles E. Bolton was just passing on his way to the Webb House at 73 Second Street. Mr. Ware called Bolton into the store, and introduced the two men, passing Morse off as a mine owner also.

"Mr. Ware tells me you are a mining expert, Mr. Bolton. I have a number of ore specimens in my office, and would appreciate it if you could accompany me there and examine them for me."

Mr. Bolton and the detective then headed downtown together — down Bush Street to Montgomery, thence via California Avenue, they reached 320 Sansome Street. There, they entered and proceeded into an office, the office of Chief Detective J. B. Hume. Black Bart knew something was wrong when the man had taken him into the Wells Fargo Building; now he realized he had been neatly trapped.

Detective Hume wasted no time in preliminaries, and stepping to a hat rack, proceeded to take from it a small derby hat, which he extended toward Mr. Bolton, with a request that he try it on.

Charles E. Bolton nonchalantly complied and then remarked, "It fits me, sir; do you wish to sell it!"

"I would hardly feel justified in trying to sell you a hat which already belongs to you, sir," replied Hume.

Bolton agreed that the handkerchief with the blood on it was his, but also stated it had been stolen from him. No, the bloodstains did not come from his skinned hand; the wound had not been caused by a rifle bullet, he had skinned it in a mine shaft. The truth of the matter was that Black Bart had skinned that hand while forcing open one of the strong boxes.

Meanwhile, an officer with a search warrant had ransacked Bolton's room, and soon appeared in Hume's office, delivering a bundle which contained a double-barreled shotgun, unbreeched, a gray linen duster, and an old Bible, in which appeared the name of Charles E. Boles, the man's real name. The Bible had been given to him by his wife when he was in the army. With such indisputable evidence placed before him, the suspect at last gave in, admitting that he was Black Bart.

"We found no ammunition in your room for the shotgun, Mr. Boles."

A sad smile flitted across the man's face as he replied, "Gentlemen, I never owned any. In all my holdups, my gun was always empty. After serving in the army, and seeing what a lot of misery a gun could bring to humanity, I swore never again to fire a gun as long as I lived, and I have kept that vow!"

Black Bart, the bold bandit, also told the officers that he never used a horse, as he had a deadly fear of the animals. The men just shook their heads in amazement. It was unreal, here was a famous western outlaw who never rode a horse or ever carried a loaded gun.

The prisoner also told the officers that he would reveal the hiding place of the gold taken from the last robbery, if the jail sentence would be made lighter.

"I cannot promise anything or make any deals," said Hume, "but it certainly will be in your favor."

Black Bart took the officers to the scene of the last holdup, and in the hollow stump, they found the five thousand dollars which he had taken. During the period of over seven years that Black Bart had operated, it is claimed that he got away with the total sum of fifty thousand dollars, but all that the company ever did recover was the sum of five thousand. What happened to the remainder of the money is a moot question, for Boles refused to discuss it with anyone, although it was rumored that he had been a victim of some slick money operators.

Taken to Mohelumne Hill, where he had robbed a stage, Black Bart was arraigned in the superior court, and on his plea of guilty-as-charged, was sentenced to serve six years in the San Quentin Prison. He was received at the California prison from Calaveras County on November 21, 1883, for the offense of robbery. When he was admitted to the prison as Convict No. 11046, Black Bart was forty-eight years old, five feet seven inches tall, with blue eyes and grey hair. He was released from custody on January 21, 1888.

Many reports were circulated that Black Bart was paid a monthly pension of two hundred dollars by Wells Fargo on his promise not to rob any more of their stages. Suffice to say, the stage robberies did not occur again.

Although many have claimed that Black Bart disappeared from the eyes of men after his release from prison, this author checked his movements with accurate results. He was seen in San Francisco for a brief time after his release; then in Cripple Creek, Colorado; then in Hannibal, Missouri. He also traveled to Mexico, Alaska, and Japan, and finally returned to his birthplace in New York, where he died in 1917.

There has been no parallel in the history of crime which can compare with that of the career of Charles E. Boles. He robbed numerous stages with an unloaded gun, and escaped each time without the aid of a horse, using only his two feet to cover great distances in a short time. Seven years a holdup man without firing a shot!

Chapter Two

Big Jim Courtright

IT WAS SPRING in Springfield, Illinois. The year was 1845 and the new season came to the little rustic town of two thousand people in all its splendor.

Roses, honeysuckle, dogwood were all in bloom, and in the surrounding woods, the violets and other wild flowers were spreading a colorful carpet beneath the trees. It was an unpretentious little town, but it loomed large in the eyes of the citizens, for it was the largest in Sangamon County, and it would loom larger in the eyes of the nation in years to come, for here dwelt Abraham Lincoln, then a country lawyer.

Spring, always a busy time in the country, seemed doubly important to Daniel Courtright, for he had another mouth to feed. A young son had been added to his family of four daughters, to which another son would be added four years later. Daniel was a hardworking farmer, frugal by nature, who feared God, read the Bible, and ruled his family with an iron hand. Frontier children were not pampered.

The boy was named Timothy Isaiah, and as all frontier boys, he was able to learn the ways of the farm at an early age. As soon as they were able to work, they carried in wood, hunted eggs, drew water and went into the fields, if for no other reason than to watch and to learn. A few years more, and then they would be doing a man's work. Timothy saw things differently. He wanted to be on his own, so when he was fifteen, he was on his way.

Timothy traveled evidently in a western direction, for he next turned up in Iowa. He was known as Tim, but somewhere about this time or a little later, Tim became Jim. What sort of work he did in Iowa is not known, but at fifteen, he was six feet tall and thin and wiry, with thick brown hair, and weighed one hundred forty-five pounds. Hard work had developed his muscles. As an experienced nimrod and an expert shot, he may have hired out as a hunter to some hotel. In those days, hunters often supplied hotels with game. It is certain that he was in Iowa, for when the Civil War broke out, he enlisted as a boy from Iowa, at the age of sixteen. It proved to be a turning point in his life. His marksmanship brought him to the attention of Gen. John Logan.

Both Logan and Courtright were wounded at the battle of Fort Donelson, Courtright evidently stopping a bullet intended for Logan, which led to a lifelong friendship, Logan ever after regarding Courtright as an intimate friend. He never lost contact after the war, during which Courtright was Logan's most trusted spy and scout. Courtright had a great admiration for Logan and probably wore his hair long to imitate the general. His work as a spy-scout was good training for his detective work years later in Fort Worth, Texas.

In July 1865, Courtright, still an army scout, was working with Wild Bill Hickok, also a Union scout. They both served near Springfield, Missouri. Many times, Jim was a dispatch rider from one outpost to another.

It was a hard and dangerous life; with the law of self-preservation uppermost in one's mind, it was the survival of the fittest. Like the mountain man, the trapper, the cowboy, and the gambler, army scouts were a breed of their own. They made love like Casanova, could track like an Indian, rode like the cowboys, and had the eyes of an eagle. In fact, the army scout was a more refined edition of the cowboy, who inherited all his virtues and mixed in a few of his vices for good measure.

It was while stationed with the army at Little Rock, Arkansas, that Jim first saw Sarah Elizabeth Weeks when he stopped at a farmhouse one day for a drink of water. Though Betty, as she was called, was only fourteen at the time, it was love at first sight for both. In the autumn of 1866, after a short courtship, they were married in Little Rock, although there is reason to believe that Jim did not take Betty from her home until perhaps a year or two later, due to the uncertain nature of army life.

This was the time when the dime novel made its appearance, fostered by writers like Ned Buntline, who caught the fancy of the public with tales of the adventures and exploits of scouts like Buffalo Bill, Hickok, and Courtright, which led to the birth of the wild west shows, featuring marksmanship, riding, roping, Indian fights, pony express ambushes, and various other phases of frontier adventures. Of these, Buffalo Bill was the most prominent.

Following his discharge from the army, about 1870, Jim and Betty joined one of these shows, but after a short time Jim took Betty back to her parents and here, in Little Rock, on October 8, 1872, their oldest child was born. After working for his father-in-law for about a year, Jim decided to try farming across the Trinity River in Texas where the Oakwood Cemetery (where Jim is buried) is now located in Fort Worth.

This venture proved unsuccessful, so Jim again turned his attention to the wild west show world. With Betty, also a crack shot, he joined Buffalo Bill's Wild West Show. At this time, the show consisted mainly of Indians, former government scouts, sharpshooters of both sexes, and stagecoach drivers. The billboard advertising featured Annie Oakley, "Little Sure-Shot," as Chief Sitting Bull called her, Lillian Smith, John C. Morgan, Betty Courtright, Jim Courtright, and several others. The show played Virginia City and while there, Jim was shot and injured by the explosion of a pad in the blank cartridge, which caused a wound on the forehead above the right eye. Jim was placed in a hospital in Virginia City.

The day following the accident, the show left town. Buffalo Bill, evidently hard-pressed for money, found it convenient to forget Jim, who was left behind without money. The citizens of Virginia City, angered at such treatment

Jim Courtright, originally known as "Tim" for Timothy, sought adventure in the great West, and found it. He once rode with Buffalo Bill's famed Wild West show, also was town marshal at Fort Worth, Texas.

After ranging far out on the frontier, even working with Wild Bill Hickok as an army scout, Jim Courtright began farming near Fort Worth, Texas. This view shows Fort Worth's Main Street looking north to the courthouse, early 1900s. Fort Worth became a hub for Courtright's varied activities.

to Courtright, took up a collection to pay Jim's hospital bill.

A rifle contest act, in which Annie Oakley, Lillian Smith, and John C. Morgan were featured, got into an argument with Buffalo Bill at this time about money due them. Lillian Smith left the show and returned to Virginia City, where she opened a shooting gallery, since at that time markswomen were quite the rage running shooting galleries.

Jim Courtright and his wife returned to Fort Worth, where he seemed more successful in politics. On April 5, 1876, he became city marshal of Forth Worth. Jim did his job well in a town where the sixgun was worn openly and used quite often. Most men settled their disputes without depending upon the law to help either way. Probably no other town in Texas boasted a more boisterous, belligerent, and devil-may-care citizenry than did Fort Worth, unless perhaps it was El Paso. Jim found many opportunities to display his speed and accuracy with a sixgun, as well as to make use of his utter fearlessness.

But all things come to an end. Perhaps Jim's army training made him a partisan of the first water. At any rate, the marshal threw his political allegiance to one faction in Fort Worth, while he should have been attending to his police duties. The party he backed lost the election; this, of course, resulted in his losing out in his bid for holding the marshal's position.

About this same time, a drama was being played in El Paso that was to involve the services of Big Jim Courtright. Capt. Jim Gillett, famed Texas Ranger, was the marshal of El Paso, and Col. A. J. Fountain of Mesilla, New Mexico, had asked him to take over the duties of town marshal in a newly-created mining camp in New Mexico, called Lake Valley.

Fountain told Captain Gillett that Lake Valley was a camp to his liking; that it was rough and tough, with something interesting happening all the time.

"I need men like you, Gillett, to keep those toughs in line."

"Sorry, colonel, but I'm getting too old for that sort of ruckus," Gillett replied. "I want to settle down and become a rancher before it is too late and I stop a bullet. But I can recommend just the man for you, Jim Courtright. Jim did a powerful good job over in Fort Worth until he got on the wrong side of the political fence. He can do you as good a job as I or anyone else could."

"Maybe I could get Wes Hardin or Ben Thompson," suggested Colonel Fountain.

Captain Gillett laughed. "Colonel, take my

word for it, Big Jim will do you a better job than those two fellows."

"With that kind of recommendation, how can I refuse to hire Courtright, if he'll come," grinned the colonel.

So, in response to a telegram sent him at Fort Worth, Jim came to El Paso, where he was introduced to Colonel Fountain by Captain Gillett. Fountain was highly impressed by the tall figure with the long dark brown hair and the steady eyes, who handled his revolvers with speed and ease.

When Jim Courtright arrived in Lake Valley, he learned that two outlaws had been making life miserable for the miners. These two men accosted Jim one evening and made the mistake of drawing against the "dude," as they called him. Too late, they realized they had made the greatest mistake of their lives. Both men wound up as residents of the newly-established "Boot Hill" cemetery.

Before long, the camp was peaceful and things began to bore Jim. But then, the mines played out and the population of Lake Valley left for greener pastures, and the place became a ghost town. Again, Jim was out of a job.

Here once more, Jim's good friend General Logan came to the rescue. The general owned a large ranch in the American Valley of New Mexico, but his profits were meager because the range was overrun with nesters and cattle rustlers. Courtright needed employment and General Logan needed a fast gun and a determined lawman to handle the situation. So Jim moved onward to the general's ranch, and began his job as foreman.

For some time, the situation in the west and the southwest had been cattlemen versus settlers. How many people were slain in the invasion of the state of Wyoming by a band of cutthroats and hired assassins in 1892 never will be known. Many lie in unmarked and unreported graves. Part of this crowning infamy was the cold-blooded and deliberate murder-hanging of Jim Averill and his wife, Cattle Kate, on the Sweetwater.

In New Mexico, Jim represented the cattlemen, so it was Courtright versus the "sod-busters," right off the reel. His was the task to rid the Logan range of the unwanted nesters

or squatters. Jim liked to earn his pay, so he gave warning to all those he said were encroaching on the general's property. The nesters, in turn, said they had legal right to this public land, but the ranchers, seeing their choice plots gobbled up by the undesired element, and their water holes diminishing, took drastic measures to correct the situation.

One day Jim and a fellow gunman, Jim McIntire, rode out to see if two Frenchmen who had squatted on a choice bit of Logan range had heeded the warning to move out. This McIntire was the same man who later wrote a book entitled *Early Days in Texas* or *Trip to Hell and Heaven*. He said that he had had a vision of being sent to hell, and that this book was the result of that dream. He also was the city marshal of Las Vegas, New Mexico, when a mob tried to take Dave Rudabaugh from the train while Dave and Billy the Kid were prisoners of Pat Garrett.

Of course, it was foolish for the two Frenchmen to buck the guns of Courtright and McIntire, so the ultimate outcome was they were killed. A universal hue and cry rose over these killings, indicating to the two Jims that it was time to leave the district. Warrants were sworn out, the charge being murder.

Courtright did not feel the necessity of leaving the country, but McIntire held the matter in a different viewpoint. He realized, more than Courtright did, apparently, that with the coming of the telegraph to this remote part of the country, outlaws and bandits were not so isolated from the people as they had been in the past. Already an officer from the Territory of New Mexico had gone to Texas to secure warrants at Austin for the arrest of Courtright and McIntire. So, it did the fugitives no good to race out of New Mexico into Texas, thinking they were safe from arrest.

John Richmond, the officer from New Mexico, saw fit not to attempt to arrest Courtright alone, but requested the assistance of Texas Rangers, Lieutenant Grimes and Corporal Hayes in so doing. Courtright believed evidently he was comparatively safe from the law while in Texas, for he came back to Fort Worth, making no secret of his presence there. So, one can imagine his surprise when, on

October 18, 1884, he was placed under arrest by the three officers.

But Jim had a lot of friends in Fort Worth. These people looked at Jim in two ways: he was the kind of a man who was either liked a great deal or disliked with the same degree of feeling. There were no in-between feelings toward Jim Courtright. Also, the town where he had served as a good marshal, was basically a cow town. It was easy to see, therefore, how the rumor got started that the nesters in New Mexico wanted Jim brought back there so they could lynch him. When the train arrived at the depot to remove Jim and his captors from Fort Worth, a large, sympathetic crowd surged upon the platform.

The newspapers, the next day, carried a brief statement that was made by Texas Adjutant General King, whom the governor had sent to Fort Worth in connection with the Courtright matter:

"An open, lawless and dangerous attempt was made by a large crowd to rescue him. This attempt failed, partly through the coolness of the two Rangers who had Courtright in charge, and partly through the efforts of Judge Hood of the District Court, Sheriff Maddox and others, who assisted in keeping the mob from an overt act of violence, and succeeded in having the prisoner conveyed to the county jail."

Courtright did not remain a prisoner very long. Sunday, the day following his arrest, he was taken to a restaurant by the officer from New Mexico, where he was rescued by a bunch of his friends. They had rushed en masse to the table and in the confusion, and unnoticed by Richmond, someone had given Jim two Colts. The Rangers also put in an appearance, but it was useless to go against those deadly revolvers in the hands of an expert.

The two Rangers, who had been instructed by Adjutant General King to act on orders from the New Mexico officer, were absolved of all guilt in the escape of Courtright. Even as it was, Richmond was charged later with misconduct and failing to listen to the advice of the Rangers, a mild reprimand to say the least, when he should have been censured severely for his carelessness and misjudgment.

Courtright bided his time. Well-schooled in the sentiments of the West, Jim later did as so many other badmen had done. With little fanfare he returned to New Mexico and surrendered to the authorities. His timing had been excellent. The witnesses were scattered or had become disinterested in the matter of the killing of the two Frenchmen. Even so, the case had to be tried. The jury consisted of men who were strangers to both Courtright and his victims; men who probably cared little about the entire matter. There was no public sentiment against Jim, a fact which also weighed heavily in his favor. He was found not guilty, and was discharged.

Oddly enough, Courtright returned to Fort Worth, where he served in many capacities in an office in an old brick building near the courthouse. The sign on his door read "T.I.C. (his full name initials) Commercial Detective Agency." Jim had conceived the bright idea of becoming the first "shake-down" artist in Fort Worth. His agency, for a monthly fee, offered "protection" to those gamblers who wished to operate in the city, in violation to certain anti-gambling ordinances which were on the books. Many decent citizens who had known Jim for years, merely shook their heads on learning of his new venture.

"He sure had come down a long way," most of them said.

It was while carrying out the duties of his agency that Jim Courtright met his nemesis in the form of Little Luke Short. Luke was a small man, never weighed over a hundred fifty pounds, and probably was about five feet five inches tall. He was also a product of the frontier, his family moving from Arkansas to Texas during the Civil War. He was an expert shot and as cool as a cucumber. He tried being a cowboy, but found the work too grueling; he wanted to make money the easy way. He even went to Nebraska, where he found a partner and began bootlegging whiskey to the Indians. He had several close calls with the army in regard to his activities, so he left Nebraska and went to Denver. There, he took up gambling and saloon-keeping; these two occupations seemed to fit Luke's makeup very well. He made the circuit from Leadville, Colorado; to Dodge City, Kansas; and thence to

Tombstone, Arizona, where he wound up dealing faro at the Oriental. It was in Tombstone that he killed a fellow gambler named Charles Storms. The incident was graphically described in the journals of one George W. Parsons, who, on February 25, 1881, wrote the following:

"Quite peaceable times lately, but today the monotony was broken by the shooting of Chas. Storms by Luke Short on the corner of Oriental. Shots, the first two were so deliberate I didn't think anything much was out of the way, but at the next shot I seized my hat and ran into the street just in time to see Storms die, shot through the heart. Both gamblers, L. S. running game at Oriental. Trouble brewing during night and morning and S was probably aggressor though very drunk. He was game to the last and after being shot through the heart by a desperate effort steading revolver with both hands fired 4 shots in all I believe. Doc Goodfellow bro't bullet into my room and showed it to me, .45 calibre and slightly flattened. Also showed a bloody handkerchief, part of which was carried into the wound by pistol. Short, very unconcerned after shooting . . . probably a case of kill or be killed. Forgot to say that the Faro games went right on as though nothing had happened after body was carried into Storms' room in the San Jose House."

In 1883 Luke returned to Dodge City, Kansas, where he fell out with the city fathers who, being jealous of his successful handling of his saloon and gambling business, ran him out of town. But Luke was not without "influential" friends. He came back with Bat Masterson and Wyatt Earp, and soon had the mayor and the sheriff eating out of his hand. Short was one of those frontiersmen who did not like to remain long in one place. So, he sold his Long Branch Saloon in Dodge City and headed for Texas, landing in Fort Worth in 1887.

Most writers have claimed that Luke owned and opened the White Elephant Saloon in Fort Worth, but this is in error. This saloon was already there when Luke arrived; it was the property of Jim Courtright and his wife, Betty. They rented it out and Jim collected the protection money from the tenants as well as the rentals. Little Luke rented a small room at the back of the saloon and set up a gambling arrangement. Of course, Jim was not long in telling Luke the setup regarding the payment of the protection money. Some people have claimed that Jim did not own the agency but was just the collection or "bagman" for the outfit, which was controlled by a number of prominent businessmen.

At any rate, Jim's fearsome reputation with a gun made him a successful collector of this money. On the night of February 8, 1887, he walked into the White Elephant Saloon, back

Little Luke Short, legendary gunman of the West, may have looked harmless when decked out in his best attire, but he was a dangerous rogue when challenged. He and Courtright finally shot it out.

Kansas State Historical Society

The White Elephant Saloon in Fort Worth was located in the 600-block of Main Street in Fort Worth. Courtright and his wife, Betty, owned and operated the famed saloon.

to the gambling room, and demanded that Short pay up the money. It was a routine matter for Big Jim, but when Little Luke told him to go to hell, that he was running an honest game and had no intention of paying tribute to any bunch of crooks, Big Jim was puzzled.

It didn't make sense, the little shrimp talking to Big Jim that way. Courtright started for his gun to give Luke a gun whipping, then changing his mind saying, "I'll be back, and, by God, you better have the money to pay!"

Jim left and Short gathered a few friends to ask for advice. Most of those present advised Luke to comply with Big Jim's demands. Then a long, lean and lanky individual spoke up in a drawling voice.

"If I was in your place, Luke, I'd trust to luck. Just take your time and don't get excited. Take your time."

Luke grinned as he replied, "That's sure good advice. I'll remember it, if I can find time."

About eight o'clock, Courtright came looking for Little Luke. A mutual friend brought Short outside the White Elephant and Luke just stood there, looking at Courtright, not saying a word, his thumbs hooked in the armholes of his vest.

"Well?" was all that Courtright said.

"Like I told you before," said Luke, "I'm not paying off. I have no intention of paying now or any other time. Is that plain enough for you, Jim Courtright?"

Luke's hands started to drop down in a natural fashion.

"Don't you pull a gun on me," cried Jim.

"I'm not trying to pull a gun, I haven't got a gun there," replied Luke.

"Don't try to trick me!" yelled Jim.

Both men went for their guns. Luke had a slight advantage, since his hand was closer to his hip, and perhaps Jim at first did believe he was unarmed. Courtright was in the act of bringing his revolver to level point when Luke fired. The bullet went wild, but caught Jim's hammer thumb in a freak quirk of fate. It was as lucky a shot as was ever made in the history of the West, and, of course, it saved Luke's life.

17

The dismayed Courtright lost no time in trying to throw his pistol from his right hand to his left hand, rather than reach for his left hand gun. However, the split-second maneuver gave Short the opportunity to drive home three more shots. One of the bullets smacked Jim directly in the heart.

A stunned silence followed. The gaping bystanders could not believe their eyes. Everyone had expected Jim to kill Luke but it was a real twist of fate. To understand the killing of Big Jim Courtright, the fastest man with a gun in Texas, by Little Luke Short, was so baffling, certain details must be told. Big Jim had his sixguns in holsters. Luke Short didn't wear a gun belt. His gun was in his hip pocket, and anybody knowing about gunfighting knows that a man with a gun in his hip pocket against a gunman with one in a holster, has about one hundred-to-one chance against him, even if the man with a holster gun is a second rater.

Big Jim Courtright was not a second rater. But he was dead. Everybody admitted he played it bad trying the "border shift," but nobody could understand how Luke Short's first bullet hit Courtright's thumb. As was said that night, "It was a mystery gunfight, sure as hell!"

As the days passed and the arguments over what happened increased, the picture became so enlarged and distorted that there was some question just where the fight took place. Those who saw it claimed it happened in the saloon. Others began to contend it took place in the street.

And what did the quiet, mannerly Little Luke have to say about all this commotion? He sat calmly in the county jail and appeared more at ease than those who arrested him. His manner did not reveal that of a desperado, but more of a demeanor of having rendered a public service, and which, no doubt, he did. Luke was known throughout the West as a sporting man, a gambler of the first rate; he never was considered the desperado or dangerous type. Luke had very little to say about it all:

"Of course, it is an affair to be regretted. If I felt I was in the wrong, I wouldn't like to talk about it, but as I wasn't, there is no reason to refrain from telling how it happened. In the first place I want to say that it was all sudden, all unexpected by me. There had been no previous disagreement between us. Early in the evening I was getting my shoes blackened at the White Elephant, when a friend of mine asked me if there was any trouble between Courtright and myself, and I told him there was nothing.

"A few minutes later I was at the bar with a couple of friends when someone called me. I went out into the vestibule and saw Jim Courtright and Jake Johnson. Jake and I had talked for a little while that evening on a subject in which Jim's name was mentioned, but no idea of a difference was entertained. I walked out with them upon the sidewalk, and we had some quiet talk on private affairs. I reminded him of some past transactions, not in an abusive or reproachful manner, to which he assented, but not in a very cordial way. I was standing with my thumbs in the armholes of my vest and had dropped them in front of me to adjust my clothing when he remarked, 'Well, you needn't reach for your gun!' and immediately put his hand on his gun and pulled it. When I saw him do that, I pulled my pistol from my hip pocket, too, and began shooting, for I knew that his action meant death. He must have misconstrued my intention in dropping my hands before me. I was merely adjusting my clothing, and never carry a pistol in that part of my dress."

After adding this mystery to the fight, Luke Short refused to make any further statements.

One would think a dignitary had come to Fort Worth and had put up in the county courthouse, the way people flocked to see the little man who had so smoothly disposed of Jim Courtright. But through it all, Luke remained as calm as though nothing out of the ordinary had occurred.

Friends of Courtright tried to come up with explanations of how Short was able to kill Courtright. He was quick as lightning, fast as a cat on his feet, a dangerous enemy all around. Courtright's friends claimed Little Luke owned his life to the very fact that Jim's gun was not in proper working order. Police officers who examined the weapon later stated that the cylinder failed to revolve. Many claimed that the entire thing had been a "frameup," and that while Jim had been drinking someone switched revolvers on him.

Luke Short appeared before Justice of the Peace Smith at 2:00 P.M. on February 9, to be examined for his part in the shooting affair. He was represented by attorneys McCart, Capps, and Steadman.

Witnesses to the fight were interviewed and their testimony recorded. Police officer Fulford reported that when he arrived at the scene of the shooting, Courtright was lying on his back and muttered to him, "Full, they've got me."

There was little doubt in the minds of all concerned but that Luke had acted in self-defense. In view of this and the testimony given, Justice Smith set Luke's bond at two thousand dollars, which was signed at once by bondsmen Jake Johnson, W. T. Maddox, Robert McCarty, and Alex Steadman.

Officer J. J. Fulford and a friend, Charles Sneed, went around Fort Worth and took up donations for Jim's widow. Many names were placed on the subscription list, again proving that in most cases, people are willing and anxious to help those in trouble and those down-and-out. Jim's widow, Betty, sold her interests in the White Elephant Saloon and left Fort Worth for California. There she lived out her life. I was fortunate to have been a close friend of Lulu May Courtright Hart, one of Jim's fine children.

What about Luke Short? He died peacefully in his bed at Queda Springs, Kansas, September 8, 1893, at the age of thirty-nine. Jim was forty-two when he died. Relatives brought Luke's body back to Fort Worth, and Jim and Luke repose in the same cemetery there, Oakwood, at Grand and Gould avenues.

End of the trail for Jim Courtright in the Oakwood Cemetery in Fort Worth.

Ironically, Jim Courtright and Luke Short, who gunned him down, lie in the same cemetery, Oakwood. Short died peacefully in Kansas in 1893; his family returned the body to Fort Worth.

Chapter Three

Bill Doolin, Train Robber

ON APRIL 22, 1889, a pistol shot was
fired that echoed throughout the southwest, for it was the signal that the fertile lands
of the vast Oklahoma Territory were opened
to a screaming, racing, land-hungry line of
thousands of immigrants. And, it was also
this land rush that brought into being the
many outlaws who infested the area, namely
the Daltons, and Bill Doolin and his crowd.

Bill Doolin was not a vicious killer, as were
many outlaws of the day; he was a deliberate,
calculating man, accurate with the sixgun and
the rifle, but not a fast draw and trick-shot
artist, as many would have us believe. He was
a man with many friends, and many enemies
. . . a man whose exploits in the robbing field
were so numerous and so expertly done that
United States Marshal Grimes and his men
were determined to rid the territory of him
and his kind.

For a long time, Bill Doolin worked at the
Bar X Bar Ranch, as well as the Turkey Track
Ranch. It was while working at the Halsell
Ranch that Doolin became acquainted with
such young men as Bill Powers, Dick Broadwell, Bitter Creek Newcomb, and several of
the Dalton brothers. And, like many of the
young men of the day, he made extra money
by selling whiskey to the Indians. One thing
led to another, and soon Bill Doolin was riding
with others of his kind, chiefly the Daltons.

An interesting facet of the gang's operations
was that they had their special "trade mark."
In every train robbery attempted by the gang,
the robbers disclosed three acts which branded

the incident as having been committed by the
Dalton-Doolin faction. First, the forcing of
the door of the express car had been done by
the fireman of the ill-fated train under compul-
sion of the guns placed at his head, a fact
made known to the messenger within which
made him hesitate to shoot from fear of hitting
the member of the train crew. Second, no attempt was made to go through the coaches
and relieve the passengers of their money and
jewels. Third, upon the leaving the scene of
their exploit, volleys were fired at the passenger cars, evidently with the intention of dis-
couraging pursuit, but with a terrible disre-
gard for the taking of human life, as the guns
were aimed at the wooden sides of the coaches
instead of at the windows, roofs or in the air.

Several days prior to their next robbery,
which occurred on May 8, 1891, Doolin and
Bob Dalton learned that the train to pass
through Wharton (now Perry), that evening
was carrying several deputy marshals, or at
least their information pipeline had told them
so. As it turned out, however, only one officer
was aboard.

At six o'clock on May 8, the bandits, Bob
and Emmett Dalton, Bill Doolin, and Charlie
Bryant, rode from their camp on Red Rock
Creek toward the train station several miles
distant. At nine-thirty, the outlaws drew rein
at their destination. They had no fear of discov-
ery, for in the hamlet were scarely a dozen
inhabitants, all told, and only three buildings,
one of which was a general store and post
office. There was a Wells Fargo Express Com-

20

pany in the small station, however, due to the business which was generated by the cattle and horse ranches in the area.

Tying their horses at the rail behind the building by the tracks, the bandits went into action. Hurriedly placing a black cloth mask over his face and pulling his hat down over his eyes, Bob Dalton crept into the station.

The agent was alone. Covering the elderly man with his rifle, the outlaw called out, "Go out and set the signal for No. 403 to stop."

"The train won't stop here," said the frightened man.

"We know it pulls through at 10:13 and it will stop if you signal it, now get going," replied Bob, raising his rifle menacingly.

But the poor agent needed no further urging. He placed his red lantern in its proper bracket; then returned to the station, where he was quickly bound and gagged.

While Bob was so engaged, the other three robbers had made a tour of the store and two houses, and found everything quiet. Returning to the station, they found Bob cutting the telegraph wires, as always was done. After assisting him, all four untied their horses and

Famed lawman Bill Tilghman was one of several who spent years running the Doolin gang to earth or prison. Tilghman was once police chief of Oklahoma City.

21

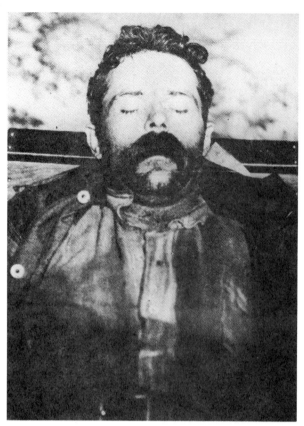

Little Dick West was one of the last of the outlaw band tracked by Bill Tilghman and a posse. He was killed on April 7, 1898.

led them to the woods, a quarter of a mile away.

There was still fifteen minutes before the train was due and these they passed in examining their rifles and revolvers and Emmett, Doolin, and Bryant put on their masks.

At last, the headlight of the Texas Fast Express on the Santa Fe route appeared, the engineer saw the red lantern, tooted his whistle as to signal to the conductor and crew that the train was to stop, and set his brakes.

As the heavy wheels slid over the rails, the four outlaws sprang from the end of the station where they had hidden. Apparently the robbers were as intent on locating the officer as they were in robbing the train. Some reports claimed that Deputy United States Marshal Chris Madsen had been aboard the train; others said it was a man named Payne. In any event, Payne's account was given as follows:

"I was asleep in my berth in the last car on the train, having retired early, as I was completely used up by my work of the preceding week. I was dreaming of my cheerful home and comfortable bed I should reach in a few hours, when I was awakened by a sudden jerk and knew the train was slowing down to stop.

"At first I thought nothing of it. Then I realized that the Texas Fast Express very rarely stopped between Arkansas City and Guthrie and the memory of the Daltons and Bill Doolin flashed through my mind. In an instant, I was at the window to see what was up.

"While I was thus engaged, two shots rang out. I knew then the train had been held up, presumably by my enemies.

"Not caring to let them pump my carcass full of lead, I sprang to the floor, ran to the rear platform, jumped to the ground and hid in some bushes.

"To my good fortune in having chosen a berth in the last car, I undoubtedly owe my life.

"From my place of concealment, I could hear the loud shouts and frightful curses of two of the bandits as they rushed the cars hunting for me. But they soon gave up their search, probably because Conductor McTaggart swore by all that was good and holy, and with admirable coolheadedness, by the way, that I nor any other marshal was not on the train and could not, therefore, leave Wichita till the next morning.

"Apparently satisfied, the two bandits rejoined their companions. I was told later that they had forced the fireman to leave the engine, and batter down the door of the express car with his coal pick though they did not afterwards shoot him down in cold blood as they had to others in the past.

"But the messenger was not quick witted and was forced to open the safe. The robbers seized a package containing $1,600 but in their haste failed to discover a sack which held $5,000. Their booty secured, the outlaws jumped from the car, fired some shots at the coaches, and darted off.

"As they went, they passed within a few yards of me. But though I had my Colt with me, I did not shoot at them. The moon made the place as bright as day, and I knew that even if I winged one or more of them, I would

The last known revolver used by outlaw Bill Doolin was this SA Frontier Army Colt, .38 cal., W.C.F., 4¾-inch barrel. The notches are cut in the right-hand grip. Shown also are the Henry Starr holster and Jack Campbell's gun belt. All saw much action in their time . . .

not stand a chance of survival against four crack shots.

"The whole affair had not taken more than half an hour. After I had seen the desperadoes disappear, I soon heard the beat of their horses' hoofs, but at the same moment I heard the brakes on the train released, and before I could gain it, it had gotten under way.

"Rushing to the station, I released the terrified agent. In a short time we had repaired the telegraph wires, and I had him send a concise account of the holdup to Wichita.

"Also, I had him send a request for men and horses to join me at Orlando, the next station, where the agent told me there were some two hundred inhabitants. When I reached there, I roused some of the people and soon an armed posses was on the march.

"At daybreak, a carload of horses and men reached the town, and from them I selected several whom I knew and to be trusted, and we set out on the trail of the bandits, a chase by the way, which lasted six weeks and ended in the death of one of my posse and also one of the outlaws."

Meanwhile, the sudden fame of the Daltons and Bill Doolin mushroomed. Barflies bragged that they knew the notorious gunmen; women threatened unruly children in the name of the outlaws; hardware stores had a boom on guns and ammunition, and newspapers daily carried their names in headlines. The daring outlaws did their best to provide the news media with plenty of material.

Bill Doolin thought robbing the train at Red Rock would be a good idea; the others quickly agreed. To make the idea more of a novelty, it was decided to rob the same train that they had held up at Wharton. Like Wharton, Red Rock contained a very few houses and was of importance only as a shipping point for the stock raisers. And, it was only twenty-six miles from Wharton.

The Texas Fast Express was scheduled to pass that station at 9:40 every night. As the engineer of the train approached the little building beside the track, on the night of Thursday, June 2, 1892, he was surprised to see the signal to stop hung out.

Seldom did the train receive passengers from Red Rock, especially during the night. As the ponderous wheels of the locomotive slid along the track past the station, six masked men sprang out and pointed their rifles at the man holding the throttle.

"Stop your train!" yelled Bill Doolin.

After taking one glance at the gun barrels, the engineer hastily obeyed.

At the first indication of the slackening of speed, the conductor had thought of a holdup.

Carl Breihan Collection
"Red Buck" George Waightman, another vicious member of the Dalton-Doolin gang, owned this gun — and used it.

Collecting his brakemen, they went out onto one of the platforms of the cars and peered ahead. Simultaneously, the masked robbers had rushed toward the engine.

"It's a holdup, all right!" gasped the conductor. "Hustle through the cars and warn the passengers not to make a move and be quiet as mice."

While the brakemen carried out these orders, the man in charge of the train discreetly sought a safe place of concealment. As on their previous raids, the outlaws took the fireman from the engine and compelled him to beat down the door of the express car, not however, until the demand to open it had been refused and several shots fired to show the messenger that it was a serious matter and no idle jest.

When the door gave way, the express agent was in a state of collapse. Without ceremony, Bill Doolin jerked him to his feet and compelled him to open the safe. Instead of finding a large amount of money, there was barely two thousand dollars. The masked men vented their rage in cursing.

As before, they refrained from going through the passenger and sleeping cars, lest a greeting of lead from the weapons of some of the occupants be given to them, instead of money and jewels. As they left the scene, the

Carl Breihan Collection
This pistol belonged to Deputy Marshal Wyckoff who chased the Dalton gang. The reward poster symbolizes his work, which included Bill Doolin. He teamed with other U.S. marshals, among them U.S. Marshal Madsen and once arrested outlaw Henry Starr.

outlaws poured a volley of shots into the coaches, again the Dalton-Doolin trademark.

Once again, the gang had escaped . . . without a shot being fired at them. Deputy marshals rode to Red Rock and trailed the outlaws into Greer County. The futile chase, which lasted ten days, was described in the *Stillwater Gazette,* on June 10, 1892:

"On June 4, Sheriff John W. Hixson of Logan County returned from the trail of the Red Rock train robbers. When he left the pursurers of the robbers they were sixty miles west of Red Rock. There were twenty-five deputies in the party and he said they would press on until the trail ended or the robbers were overtaken. United States Marshals Payne and Madsen were in the Panhandle country at that date with a posse of men watching to prevent their escape. The two posses are now pursuing a northerly course through the Strip. A party has started out from Caldwell, Kansas, going south, in sufficient numbers and fully armed, to do good battle in case they intercept the fleeing road agents. It seems, beyond doubt now, that the robbers are none other than the Daltons and their colleagues, as has been generally believed since the robbery. The latest reports are that the robbers were on the trail leading to Fort Supply and their pursuers were following them very close. A posse had started from Fort Supply to intercept them. A hard fought battle may be expected at any time. It is to be hoped that this band of ruffians may receive a lesson that will deter others from attempting to follow their example.

It is known that five brothers of this now notorious family of criminals are in this territory along with an aged mother. The mother lives near King-

Bob Dalton, shown here with his sweetheart, Eugenia Moore, was one of five brothers wanted all over the West for train robberies, bank holdups and killings. The gang was described as a "notorious family of criminals."

Jay Doolin Meek

This matching watch and case belonged to outlaw Bill Doolin.

25

fisher, on a claim. Some days ago, Bill, the oldest of the boys, returned to his mother from California, where he has recently been acquitted of the charge of train robbery in that section. Bob and Emmett are also wanted by the Golden State authorities for holding up a passenger train there some years ago, and their guilt is positively known. Grattan, or Grat, as he is known among his pals, is an all around cattle and horse thief and robber of stage coaches. With the exception of Charley, who lives near Kingfisher, the family of sons are known to have committed every crime from imposing upon younger school mates at school up to robbing their defenseless fellow men after they became older . . . Bill Doolin is also one of the robbers, cautious and daring . . .

Roy Daugherty was a member of the Doolin gang who was captured in the famous fight at Ingalls. He was sent to the territorial prison at Lansing, Kansas.

Courtesy Charles Rosamond

As time went by, the gang became bolder and bolder. At last it was decided to rob two banks at the same time at Coffeyville, Kansas. It was to be carried out by the three Daltons, Bob, Grat, and Emmett; Bill Doolin, Dick Broadwell, and Bill Powers. The event was set for Wednesday, October 5, 1892. Doolin, generally conceded to be one of the shrewdest holdup artists who ever lived, was with them when they started, but he turned back, pretending his horse had thrown a shoe. Doolin felt the Daltons were headed for their Waterloo. He was right!

The destruction of the Dalton gang at Coffeyville left Bill Doolin to carry on the tradition he had begun some years before. When in full swing, the Doolin band consisted of Doolin, Bill Dalton, Bitter Creek Newcomb, Charlie Pierce, Roy Dougherty, alias Arkansas Tom, Bill Raidler, Little Dick West, Oliver Yountis, Tulsa Jack Blake, and "Red Buck" (George) Waightman, the most vicious of the lot.

The holdup of the Missouri Pacific train at Caney, Kansas, on October 14, 1892, was Bill Doolin's first job after the Coffeyville affair. At 10:15 A.M. Doolin, Bill Dalton, and Bitter Creek stepped aboard the baggage car. The express messenger, J. Maxwell, had witnessed the uncoupling of the express car from the rest of the train, so he made ready to resist the approach of the robbers. However, the continual barrage of rifle bullets through his car shortly changed his mind.

The Doolin bunch next held up the Spearville, Oklahoma, bank on November 1, 1893. It was the very next day after this robbery that Oliver Yountis was killed by officers at his home near Orlando.

Other robberies occurred, and business was good. But the fight at Ingalls, Payne County, Oklahoma, on September 1, 1893, was the beginning of the end. Three officers were killed during that red-letter-day fight, and Roy Dougherty was captured. Roy was later killed by officers when resisting arrest in Missouri, suspected of another bank robbery.

The whole bunch was at the holdup of the Rock Island train at Dover, Oklahoma Territory, on April 3, 1895 . . . but the safe refused

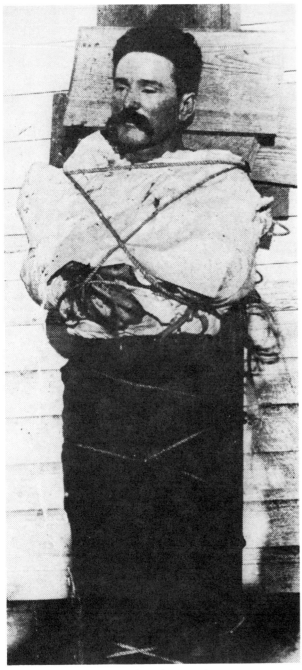

The body of George "Red Buck" Waightman, among the cruelest of the Dalton gang, was propped up on a slab after he was slain March 5, 1896 by a posse led by Chris Madsen.

Courtesy Jay Doolin Meek
Bill Doolin married Edith Ellsworth in 1893, settling for a time at Ingalls. This rare photo of Edith was taken in 1926.

to give way. In their frustration, several of the robbers compelled a black porter to go through the cars with a grain sack, relieving the passengers of their valuables. Shortly thereafter, Tulsa Blake was killed in a running fight with a posse.

Bill Doolin had married Edith Ellsworth on March 15, 1893, settling at Ingalls for a time, moving around as it became necessary to elude the law. They had one son named Jay Doolin, who later took the name of Meek, his step-father.

Doolin's band was broken up in 1895, but there was to be no peace for him, as lawmen Bill Tilghman, Chris Madsen, Heck Thomas, and Jim Masterson kept up a constant search for the one-time members of the band. Most of the outlaws had been accounted for; only Little Dick West, Bill Doolin and Bill Dalton were missing.

On June 8, 1894, Bill Dalton was killed from ambush at his home near Ardmore, Oklahoma, by Deputy Marshal Loss Hart. Dick West was killed on April 7, 1898, on the ranch of Herman Arnett, near Guthrie.

Bill Doolin, suffering from rheumatism,

27

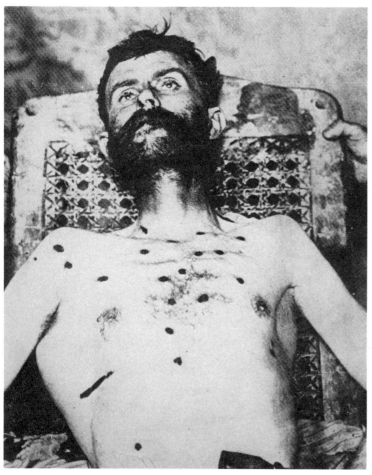

Bill Doolin was tracked to a cabin near Lawson, Oklahoma, where lawmen found him with his wife and baby son. Ordered to surrender, Doolin pulled up his rifle and was blasted by a posse.

guns rent the air, and Doolin fell, riddled with a full charge of buckshot. The date: August 25, 1896. The Dunn brothers had fired their shotguns before being ordered to do so. One bullet from Thomas' rifle also struck Bill.

A spot near the heart of the Summit View Cemetery was chosen for the last resting place of the noted bandit. His widow and Sam Trimble were the only mourners at the grave. Before burial on the twenty-eighth, Doolin's body was placed on exhibition at the Rhodes Undertaking Parlor on Oklahoma Street in downtown Guthrie.

During the next sixty-three years, Doolin's grave was marked with a twisted, rusty buggy axle. In 1959, a more suitable marker was erected on the spot.

On February 14, 1897, Mrs. Edith Doolin went to visit his wife, who was hiding in the Indian territory on a ranch near Burden, Kansas. From that point Doolin traveled to Arkansas, where he used the facilities of the hot springs to relieve his ailment. On December 5, 1895, he was arrested at the Basin Hotel by Deputy United States Marshal Bill Tilghman without a shot being fired.

In January 1896, Doolin managed to escape from the jail at Guthrie. But his fantastic escape was to no avail. He was located finally near Lawson (now Quay), Oklahoma. Heck Thomas and his men rode to the Doolin cabin in the woods in Payne County. One evening they saw Doolin leave with his wife and baby. Doolin walked in front of the wagon, examining the trail. Heck Thomas stepped out of the tall grass and ordered the outlaw to surrender. Doolin jerked his Winchester to his shoulder. Before he could fire, however, the blast of shot-

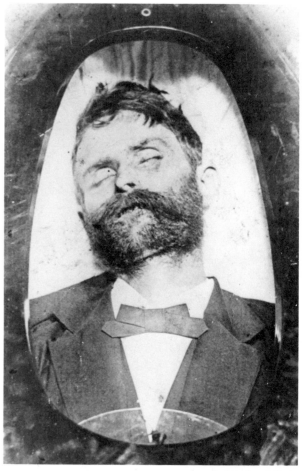

Carl Breihan Collection
End of the trail had been reached; Bill Doolin lies in his casket.

and Col. Samuel M. Meek were married in Clarkson, Oklahoma Territory. Later, with Jay Doolin, Bill's only child, they moved to Ingalls, where the boy attended school. In 1902 the family moved to Beaver County, where Colonel Meek died on July 2, 1917. When World War I broke out, Jay (using the name of Meek), enlisted in the army and saw service in France. When Jay returned from the war, he moved to Ponca City with his mother. She died in 1928 and is buried there.

For well over fifty years, Jay's true identity was unknown to the general public. He always used the name of Jay D. Meek. Jay married in Ponca City and raised a family of five children there. I am grateful that I was able to call him a friend.

Doolin's last resting place was Summit View Cemetery at Guthrie, Oklahoma.

Edith Doolin Meek later remarried. Bill Doolin's lone son survived and was known by the author.

Courtesy Jay Doolin Meek

Chapter Four

Al Jennings, Outlaw Who Ran for Governor

THE CIVIL WAR was well into its third year, leaving many of the proud, belligerent, slave-holding families of Virginia in a quandry as to what their next move should be. Federal troops were ever marching nearer to their homes, and many people believed it wise to leave Virginia.

Among those so deciding was the family of Judge Jennings. He moved his family to a plantation in Tennessee. For a time, it appeared to have been a good move, but when Gen. James Longstreet and his Confederate

Corps invaded Tennessee to attack Gen. Ambrose Burnside at Knoxville, it was decided that the Jennings family should return to their home in Virginia. The elder Jennings was assisting a Virginia regiment as a doctor when he sent word to his wife to abandon their Tennessee plantation.

On November 29, 1863, General Longstreet's army attacked Fort Sanders, where the Army of the Ohio was bravely holding out, awaiting aid from Gen. U. S. Grant. During the terrible bombardment, Mrs. Jennings and

Al Jennings who worked both sides of the law led an adventuresome life and later wound up in Hollywood as a consultant to "westerns" and a writer.

Carl Breihan Collection

Judge Jennings who hailed from Virginia was Al Jennings'
father.

her children were forced to seek refuge in an
abandoned schoolhouse. Here Alphonso J.
Jennings, the runt of the family, was born.
The back-and-forth skirmishes made it impossible for Mrs. Jennings to travel, so she remained living in the schoolhouse until the
end of the war, when her husband returned
safely.

When Al Jennings was eleven years old, his
mother died, leaving Judge Jennings with four
young sons and a daughter. John was the
eldest, followed by Edward, Frank, and Al.
Leaving Virginia, the Jennings went to Ohio,
where, near Manchester, Al ran away from
home after a quarrel with his father. Some
claim it was just a trivial matter; others state
that Al became incensed when his father killed
his pet squirrel for one reason or another.

The "Tom Thumb" sized lad went to Cin-
cinnati and then on to St. Louis. In the me-
tropolis city of Missouri, he worked at several
jobs. At a variety club, he played the trombone
for a week or so, being able to read music
after a fashion and being rather musically in-

clined. Swept ever westward in the flood tide
of migration to the new frontier, young Al
became attached to a covered wagon party
going to Colorado. Upon reaching Trinidad,
the wagon train dispersed, leaving Al alone
in that wild and woolly Colorado town, with
nothing in his pockets.

While in Trinidad, a rancher named Jim
Stanton developed a liking to the little
towheaded kid and took him under his wing.
He taught Al how to rope, run cattle, shoot
a pistol and a rifle with skill and accuracy, as
well as treating the lonely boy as a son. It was
difficult for Al to say goodbye to his close
friend Stanton, ramrod of the 101 Ranch, but
it had to be done. Al drifted around Colorado
and New Mexico for several years, deciding
then to return to see his family, now living in
West Virginia.

Al's father, a successful schoolteacher, Meth-
odist minister, lawyer, and editor, wanted Al
to follow in his footsteps, as did the young
man's brothers. Al Jennings set his mind to
it. He read law books, trying to settle his
restless nature. Finally, through the influence
of Judge Virgil Armstrong, Al entered the
University of West Virginia. He was more than
an average student. His diversified background
made him "one of his kind" at the college.
After two years of law study, Al decided to go
west again to join his father and brothers, who
had also done so. With him went his law-
student brother, Frank.

At Coldwater, Kansas, Al and Frank
Jennings were admitted to the bar. Al didn't
remain in Kansas long, but went to Boston,
Colorado, Las Animas County, where a political power struggle was going on to cut the
county in two, thus creating another county,
of which Boston was to be the county seat.
The state assembly voted for the division of
Las Animas County, but the governor vetoed
the bill. It was just as well, for there was a
fire at Boston soon after which virtually destroyed the entire settlement.

Al was disgusted with Boston; not so his
brother, Frank. Al decided to return to Oklahoma after 1889 when the land was opened
to immigrants, but Frank decided to remain
in Colorado. Frank, quite the opposite of runty

Al Jennings broke with his father and traveled to Colorado with a wagon train. He quit the train at Trinidad, stayed awhile, and then drifted.

Al, was tall and athletic. He didn't possess the hairtrigger temper that Al displayed, but was calm and collect. He became involved eventually in Colorado politics and held the position of deputy county clerk.

Al Jennings returned to Oklahoma, waiting for the opportune time to apply his knowledge as an attorney. After roaming the territory for some months, he finally settled in El Reno, where he hung out his shingle for business. Canadian County was in the throes of reorganization, so Al applied his talents in that direction for a time. He grew popular with the people, and was elected Canadian County attorney in 1892. Al did a good job as county prosecutor and brought to justice many men who deserved prison terms. His reputation as a gunman also stood him in good stead. It is said that he shot and killed a number of badmen while in his official capacity.

Failing to gain the nomination two years later, Al drifted to Woodward, Oklahoma, where his brothers John and Ed were practicing law. Al's father was also residing there, acting in the capacity of county judge. Also living in Woodward was a prominent lawyer named Temple Houston, the son of famous general United States Senator Sam Houston, liberator of the Republic of Texas.

There are several trains of thought as to how Al Jennings actually became an outlaw. Some claim that the Jennings boys — Al, John, and Edward — were resentful of Houston and Jack Love because the latter had wrested the political power in Woodward from them. Others claim that it all started over a court case when Ed Jennings called Houston a damned liar in the courtroom. Still others said Al called Temple Houston a liar, and that Ed had walked up and slapped Houston in the face.

In any event, that very evening Temple Houston strode into Garvey's saloon where John and Ed Jennings were playing cards. Some witnesses stated that Houston was drunk; that when Ed and Houston saw each other, guns started booming. John fell before he could use his own pistol. Ed dropped to the floor, dying. Al was quickly notified at his home, and he rushed to the saloon, dazed at the news. It was reported later that Ed Jennings had been shot twice — once in the

Kansas State Historical Society
Al and Frank Jennings were admitted to the bar at Coldwater, Kansas. He stayed a time, then went to the Rockies again.

left ear and once in the back of the head. Again there were conflicting reports, as in the case of many other such shootouts. Some even said that Frank Jennings was there, as well as Al.

Frank Jennings did not appear in Woodward until after the funeral for Ed. John had been seriously wounded in the affray, but recovered. Poor Judge Jennings was beside himself with grief at the death of his son.

Houston pleaded self-defense, and in a memorable trial, during which virtually all participants came to the courtroom armed, he was acquitted of the charge of murder. Embittered by the verdict, Judge Jennings moved to Tecumseh, Oklahoma, and Al and Frank Jennings decided to ride the outlaw trail in an effort to kill Temple Houston. However, fate prevented Al and Houston from meeting after that. Houston and Jennings were both

good gunfighters and there is no doubt had they met again, a fatal gunfight would have ensued.

In the spring of 1896, an attempt was made to rob the Santa Fe passenger train at Edmond, Oklahoma, near the water refueling tank. It was a disappointment for the robbers since there was no gold in the express car, nor anything else of value. All they found were several packages in new one dollar bills, probably amounting to less than five hundred dollars.

The robbers? It was learned later that Al and Frank Jennings, Pat and Morris O'Malley (brothers), and Little Dick West had pulled the job. Al went to visit his father in Tecumseh, while the others rode to the home of Laury Whipple in Pottawatomie County. There was another Whipple family who had aided outlaws previously, among them Bill Dalton,

Oklahoma Historical Society
Oklahoma was a frontier when Al Jennings came there. This is a street scene at Woodward.

33

Oklahoma Historical Society

Al and Frank Jennings formed their own robber-gang near Edmond, Oklahoma, far removed from the activities of this Edmond girls' marching band.

Bill Doolin, and other members of the Dalton family. This was the J. N. Whipple place near Meade, Kansas, then owned by Whipple and his wife, the former Eva Dalton, sister of Grat, Bob, Bill, and Emmett. The house stands today about as it was back in 1887, when it provided a handy hideout for outlaws on the run. The hand-dug tunnel which runs from the house to the barn provided a quick getaway route, when the bandits were surprised in the house. In 1940 the Meade Chamber of Commerce acquired the site for a city park, the grounds were landscaped, and the tunnel was reconstructed and walled with stone. Thousands of people from all over the world visit this historic site; this author would suggest to the reader a similar visit to the Meade-Dalton hideout.

Leaving his father's house, Al rode to the Whipple home, where he met other members of the gang. Several weeks later, the make-shift outlaw band tried to hold up the M. K. & T. train at Bond Switch, some twenty miles south of Muskogee, Oklahoma. But the railroad ties

Oklahoma Historical Society

The business block in El Reno, Oklahoma, about 1903.

34

Frontier and Old West times made familiar scenes like this in early-day Oklahoma, where Indians gathered in 1890.

piled high on the track did not frighten the brave engineer. He poured on the steam and rolled right through the barricade. It was another crude and unsuccessful job on the part of the Jennings gang.

Other stupid moves followed. The gang was thwarted in an attempt to rob a train near Purcell by a posse who had been informed of the move. The bank at Minco looked like a good prospect. Al sent Pat O'Malley into town to check things out. He returned and stated the place looked like an armed camp during

the Civil War. This move had been anticipated by deputy United States marshals, and again the plans of the gang turned to naught.

Al obtained money from some source, probably from his father. He went to Central America and Mexico for awhile, then returned to the states, again assembling his old gang members. It was difficult to rob a train with marshals Ledbetter, Tilghman, Madsen, and others on their trail.

Al Jennings decided next to hold up the Rock Island train in daylight at a point be-

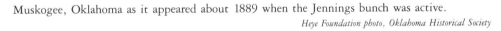

Muskogee, Oklahoma as it appeared about 1889 when the Jennings bunch was active.

tween Minco and Chickasha, where some track laborers were repairing some of the rails. The bandits compelled the foreman to station himself in such a position so that he could wave down and stop the oncoming train. After the train had stopped, conductor Dan Dacy found himself staring into the barrel of a .45 pistol, cocked. One robber leaped into the engine cab, where he took control of the engineer and fireman, while the remaining outlaws rushed to raid the express car.

The express messenger convinced Al Jennings and Dick West finally that he did not possess the keys for the two safes so they used dynamite to force them open. Another bust; the explosion shattered the smaller safe and splintered the express car. The larger safe remained upright and unopen.

"Dammit!" cried Al. "We'll have to rob the passengers to get anything out of this farce."

This the robbers did, netting only a few hundred dollars in cash and jewelry. Unfortunately for Al, his mask had slipped off, and he was recognized by the conductor as well as by the members of the train crew.

The Jennings gang, at previous times, had taken refuge at the Spike-S Ranch, property of John Harless, situated near the junction of Snake and Duck creeks in the Creek Nation. Harless was a rustler, who also took outlaws and other wanted men and protected them at his ranch, for the right price. Jennings realized that all routes to the Spike-S would be watched after the abortive Rock Island robbery, so his band wandered around the territory, resting in the woods or convenient dugouts they found.

On the night of November 29, the posse under Deputy Marshal Ledbetter located the Jennings gang at the Hereford Ranch. It was almost impossible to make a surprise attack, since the main house stood in a position with a mile of open prairie between it and the officers. The posse attempted to steal up to the house on foot. They had not advanced too far when Ledbetter saw the outlaws escaping from the ranchhouse. They had left their own worn-out mounts in the barn and had commandeered a covered wagon, in which to make a run for it.

About midnight on November 30, 1897, the bandits rode up to the Spike-S ranchhouse. The two O'Malley boys and Al Jennings needed food and rest. Little Dick West was not with them. He had decided to go it alone soon after the train robbery. Mrs. Harless answered the door.

"Welcome, Bud and Frank are here, but Dick West has not appeared. Come in, you must be nearly frozen in this wind."

"Where's John?" asked Al.

"He's in jail for changing brands again. My brother Dutch is here and so is a neighbor friend, Miss Ida Hurst."

The next morning, Al Jennings decided to leave the Harless place. Mrs. Harless expressed concern that her brother had not returned from going to the well near the barn for a bucket of water. He was in no condition to return. About five o'clock in the morning, Ledbetter and his men had surrounded the ranchhouse and were waiting for daylight. When Dutch walked toward the stable, he was promptly captured and securely tied in the barn.

Finally, Mrs. Harless threw a shawl over her head and went to find her brother. Ledbetter called to her and informed her of the circumstances. He told her to have the Jennings gang surrender, and for her and Miss Hurst to seek shelter in a graveyard over the hill from the house.

Mrs. Harless carried the news to Al. Five minutes later, she and her friend were hightailing it toward the cemetery for safety. Bud Ledbetter had deployed his men carefully. He and Payton Talbot had taken a position behind an old log cabin a short distance from the house; Thompson and his son were placed in a thicket to the northwest; Jake Elliott was put behind a stone wall near the barn, and Lon Lewis hid inside the barn.

Bullets fell like hail upon the house. Heavy calibre steel-jacketed bullets ripped through the parts of the house not made of heavy logs. The Jennings gang was in a desperate predicament.

Al Jennings pumped a load of bullets into the log cabin, behind which Ledbetter and Talbot were stationed. One bullet struck Ledbetter in the shoulder; another struck the calk-

These four judges helped mold frontier life during early days at Shawnee, Oklahoma. Al Jennings' father is on the right.

ing between the logs, showering a cloud of dust into Talbot's eyes.

"Now's the time!" cried Al. "Out the back door and into the orchard!"

Jack Elliott was the only man who saw the bandits leave the house. He fired but missed. He tried in vain to eject a jammed casing from his rifle, to no avail. He waited nearly ten minutes before advising the other men that their quarry had flown. No one knows why he waited so long, but probably he was afraid to brave that hail of lead coming from other points around the house.

It was later determined that two hundred eighty bullet holes were counted on the north side of the house. Frank Jennings had twenty bullet holes through his clothing, and Al Jennings had been wounded twice in the knees.

The next day the fleeing outlaws, with no horses, commandeered a wagon driven by two Indians. Al was unable to walk well at that point, so it was decided to stop at the home of Sam Baker, a supposed friend, for medical

attention. From there, it was decided to ride to the home of Benny Price, a friend who would harbor them. Sam Baker hurried into Checotah to warn Marshal Ledbetter of the presence of the Jennings band. Hoping to receive a handsome reward for his betrayal of the outlaws, Baker concocted a plan to ambush them on the pretext of taking them to a safer hiding place.

It seems unusual that Al Jennings and his men would trust Sam Baker to any extent; they were all suspicious of him and always had been. Yet, in their weakened and sometimes delirious condition, it is not surprising that they were willing to grasp at any offered straw. The outlaws assembled in a covered wagon and drove into an ambush. Bud Ledbetter and his men were concealed on a bluff on the east side of the river ford. Previously, the lawmen had placed a tree along the river edge to block the trail. Near the place of ambush Baker departed, stating that he must return home.

Frank Jennings then drove the wagon to-

37

ward the creek. As planned, the wheels struck the tree and the vehicle stopped. Before the outlaws could come to their senses, the wagon was surrounded by a number of men pointing rifles at the occupants.

The Jennings were brought to Muskogee by wagon and by train, where they were lodged in the hotel, under heavy guard. After the other two prisoners had been brought in, Al, Frank, and the O'Malley boys were tossed into a jail cell at Muskogee. Little Dick West was later shot and killed by federal officers while resisting arrest.

The trial at Chickasha was a sensational one, to say the least. United States Attorney W. B. Johnson was in charge of the prosecution. The brothers A. C. Cruce and W. I. Cruce, splendid attorneys, volunteered to defend Al Jennings without charge, due to their friendship with the outlaw's father. Al Jennings took the witness stand in his own defense, giving a startling and spell-binding account of his life and the circumstances thereof, dwelling on the fact that he wished to avenge his brother's murder. All this was to no avail. Al was convicted on charges of assault with intent to kill, and was sentenced to five years in the Leavenworth Penitentiary. Before the sentence could be invoked, however, Al, as well as the O'Malley brothers and Frank Jennings, were indicted on a more serious charge, robbing the United States mails, an offense which then carried an automatic life sentence to be imposed.

The jury was not long in finding Al Jennings guilty as charged, the judge taking less time to announce the sentence as being life imprisonment in the federal prison at Columbus, Ohio.

Al Jennings entered prison as convict No. 31539, seemingly having lost all hope of ever being a free man again. But this time Al had a little luck. Frank Jennings and the O'Malley boys were slated for trial the next term of court. Before that time, however, they suggested that if Judge Townend and the United States Attorney would recommend that Al's sentence be commuted to five years, they would plead guilty and also accept the same sentence. This proposition was accepted,

strangely enough. President William McKinley commuted Al's life sentence to five years. He served his time and returned to Oklahoma, only to be arrested again and placed in Leavenworth to served the five year sentence for assault. His friends renewed their activities in his behalf, and he soon walked out, a completely free man. Al's complete pardon was given him by President Theodore Roosevelt.

Frank Jennings and the O'Malley brothers returned to Oklahoma after serving their sentences and led respectful and useful lives. After his release from Leavenworth, Al began to practice law again, this time at Lawton, Oklahoma. However, politics were of keen interest to the former outlaw. In 1912 he filed and won the Democratic nomination for prosecuting attorney of Oklahoma County, over six other candidates. Before the primary, five of the candidates withdrew to concentrate the vote against him, but despite this, Al won the nomination. At the general election, he was defeated by a narrow margin by a Republican who was supported by both Republican and Democrat organizations.

But the ambitious and resourceful Al Jennings was not entirely through with politics. In 1914 he filed for the office of governor of Oklahoma.

"I am entering the race," said Mr. Jennings, "as a Democrat. Many of my friends have urged me to seek an independent nomination, but I have always been a Democrat. My object is to clean up the party in Oklahoma. I intend to fight double-dealing political thieves, with whom no self-respecting outlaws of former years can associate."

Then the ambitious Al added more to his talk:

"All I want is to see absolutely honest men at the head of the government, and after I have announced my candidacy, if some man whose integrity and uprightness are unquestioned becomes a candidate, I shall withdraw and support him with all of my ability.

"Some people do not seem to be able to understand how an outlaw, an ex-train robber and federal prisoner can become sincerely law-abiding and a reformer in politics, but the explanation is simple. I made a mistake and defied the law. I was caught and punished, kept five years in prison, and then saw how I had been wrong to become an enemy of society. I decided to reclaim my place in society and set about doing it. As soon as I became a free man, living in a free community, I began to appreciate the differences in lawbreaking and the consequences thereof, and that made me a political reformer.

"I had been a train robber, a crude, open defier of society, and I had been caught and punished. I saw all about me men who wore the best clothes and stood high in society, robbing the people right and left and not getting caught or being punished. They were not as primitive as I had been in the method they chose. They did things in the dark and only appeared in the open when they had on their Sunday clothes, so to speak."

Much to the consternation of the Democratic Party, Al Jennings polled 21,732 votes, as opposed to 33,605, the total primary vote given to Supreme Court Justice Robert L. Williams, the favorite candidate of the party. Williams won the general election by a vote of 100,904 to that of 95,904 for his Republican opponent.

"You know," said Al, after the primary, "I believe I would have won, but I was counted out of it."

Jennings later married and moved to California, where he got into the movies as an adviser and writer. Al made a lot of money and he lost a lot of money. Finally, with what he had left, he bought an acre of ground around Tarzana and started raising chickens. Up to his death a few years back, he lived comfortably on his old age pension and what little money he had managed to save.

Former outlaw Al Jennings certainly was a living example of his own keen theory on prisoner rehabilitation. He summed it up this way:

When an oldtimers' convention was held in 1937, this trio posed for an historic photograph. Al Jennings is in the center. On the left is former U.S. Marshal E. D. Nix; Chris Madsen is on the right. Their ages totaled 236 years — Nix was 76, Jennings 74 and Madsen 86.

"The greatest power in the world is the power of truth; next is the power of not being afraid."

Author's Note: I am indebted to my old friend, Fred Pottoroff of Kansas, for his kindness and patience in providing me with some notes dealing with his relative, Al Jennings; also for having introduced me to Al at his home in 1957. The old outlaw was past ninety then, but spry and cocky. His book, "Beating Back," is a good one, and I appreciate the fact that he gave me a copy. He also signed it for me, on the same page where Bat Masterson had signed his name.

Only two of the old clan were left, Al Jennings and the lone train robber, Bill Carlisle. Al would often say he was the last of the badmen, to which Carlisle would retort, "T'aint necessarily so!" The passing of time proved Bill to be right.

Al Jennings, second last of the badmen, died just before Christmas 1961, surviving his beloved wife, Maude, by one month. She passed away in November 1961, age 80. Al was 98 when he died.

Bill Carlisle passed away one warm Friday in June 1964. He was aged 74 years. Bill is buried in the Riverview Cemetery in Wilmington Delaware, in the family plot.

40

Chapter Five

Emilio Kosterlitzky, the Mexican Cossack

THE CRIMSON RAYS of sunset danced along the horizon like bucket-flung rubies against a swaying curtain of alabaster. Its blood-red curtain lifted ever so slightly, seemingly anxious to sink behind the distant hills and to shut out the grisly scene it spotlighted along the lonely Mexican road. The fading crimson haze was replaced by a slight breeze, sinister and foreboding. A single Mexican peon trudged the dusty road towards the village several miles to the south. A slight sound had caught his attention, and he looked closely to the side of the road where a few scrub trees were growing.

"Madre de Dios!" he cried, as he made the sign of the cross and struck out pell-mell down the road as if the devil himself were behind him.

The sight which had caused the man to bolt in fear was not uncommon in Mexico in those revolution days. What he had seen were five bodies hanging from the limbs of the trees, swaying gently in the soft evening breeze as if beckoning him to join them. Tacked to one of the trees was a crude sign which read "Who molests these bodies will receive the same treatment."

Arizona Historical Society

Col. Emilio Kosterlitzky, Russian-born and raised, jumped ship in the New World and later became an important figure in the Mexican Revolution.

Emiliano Zapata, famed Indian leader, was a key figure in the Mexican Revolution. He was also a close friend and associate of Pancho Villa. Years later, an outstanding motion picture was made of his life, the script written by Noble Prize-winning author John Steinbeck.

Typical soldier of Zapata's band in Mexico's revolutionary battles.

The frightened Mexican finally reached the half-sleeping village, but he cried his news by shouting, "Five banditos are hanging on the trees down the road."

And, as the sign had suggested, no one bothered the bodies but the buzzards and the elements, until nothing remained but the skeletons.

Such was one of the methods Col. Emilio (E.K.) Kosterlitzky used in disposing of bandits and enemies of the state.

Kosterlitzky was born in 1853, the son of a famous Cossack cavalryman, whose valor during the Crimean War had brought fame to this name in Moscow, Russia. The boy's father cared little about his son's following in his footsteps, so he enrolled him in the St.

Petersburg Military College. From there, he attended the Royal Naval School in the capital city. But in a sense, the young man hated water, so-to-speak, and bided his time. In September 1872, he and his shipmates were on a student voyage on a Russian battleship, when Kosterlitzky deserted his comrades at Puerto Cabello, Venezuela. The date, December 3, 1872.

Still intent on becoming a cavalryman, and learning that Mexico offered great chances in such a venture, Kosterlitzky went to New York and then to the state of Sonora, Mexico, arriving there in April 1873.

From 1873 to 1885, Kosterlitzky had worked his way up in the Mexican army to the rank of captain. He had also married the daughter of the powerful Torres family. The Torres clan ruled Sonora with an iron fist and were staunch supporters of President Porfirio

Diaz. It was also during this time that he had met a young American captain named Adna Chaffee (later a general) in Arizona, and was to meet him again in later years under different circumstances.

While his commanding officer, Col. Juan Fenochio, and his influential in-laws could have landed a soft job for Kosterlitzky in President Diaz's organization, their commendations were not altogether necessary. Dicator Porfirio Diaz recognized quickly the ability which Kosterlitzky displayed. When he organized his Guardia Rurales, he appointed the Russian colonel in command of the Northern District of Mexico. Colonel Kosterlitzky, being well educated, spoke German, Polish, Spanish, and English, as well as his native Russian. This knowledge of the languages was a boon to the colonel, for he was able to converse fluently with all concerned, as well as exercise his rigid military training to handle the outlaws and Ladrones which made up the group of Rurales.

Kosterlitzky had been raised with a member of the ruthless and bloodthirsty Russian Cossacks. Life to him was cheap and he was instilled with a devotion to his superiors, regardless of whom it involved. Not through fear did his men follow him and obey him, but through respect for his knowledge and ability. His rule was never questioned, and he ruled the entire population of the district, rich and poor alike, and in his hands rested their fate. He could arrest, try and sentence at his own discretion. Some men were turned over to his firing squad, to be placed against an adobe wall and shot to death. Sometimes he freed his prisoners. To all he was known as Juez de Cordado, "Judge of the roped ones." As ruthless as Colonel Kosterlitzky was, he gave his full loyalty to his new "czar," President Diaz.

When a prisoner was brought before Kosterlitzky, he faced both judge and jury. There was no lawyer to speak in the prisoner's behalf, no one to suggest the man might be innocent. Kosterlitzky's decision was final, regardless of what that decision might be. Under his command, his men willingly and eagerly slaughtered outlaws and disloyal Mexicans by the hundreds. He proved himself a protector of the helpless; to the peons as well, for he was always polite to them and willing to listen to their complaints. If their troubles were the doings of some arrogant public official, he saw to it that the person responsible was quickly put in his place.

"Continue such tactics and out you go," he would tell them. Well, they knew what he meant, so the offender always stopped his troublemaking quickly.

He was the soldier at all times. Always, he wore his hair in the close, clipped Russian style, and stood at attention whenever he spoke to anyone, regardless of the person's standing in life. He wore a beautiful sword at his side at all times, and when he drew it, someone knew he was going to die. The colonel never drew his sword without using it on some unfortunate person. Such a man made enemies. Many attempts were made on his life, but every time, Kosterlitzky managed to escape. Never was he known to allow even one of his most trusted men to get behind his back. When he dined, his back was always to a wall. The colonel never placed his entire confidence in anyone.

When traveling over his domain, he did so in an old Concord coach purchased from the United States Army surplus, and drawn by four magnificent horses. His coach was fitted with a bed, and there was always a supply of liquor and good food aboard the coach. Kosterlitzky believed it was easier and safer to use such a coach than to ride horseback through his district. With him went his body servant, a Mexican surgeon, an extra coach as an ambulance, and a corps of hospital personnel.

His Rurales were trained to instant obedience, and regardless of the nature of any order he issued, his men always obeyed. Every man in his outfit was given a fine horse, a service uniform of dark gray whipcord, with the tight-legged trousers having a black stripe of braid down the sides. For special occasions, each man wore his Charro outfit made of fine brown leather; also a high crowned sombrero with the Mexican insignia of eagle and serpent on it.

For their services, these hard-faced men received a good wage and took great pride in their occupation. These were hardhearted men who rode under Colonel Kosterlitzky, but such was the type of man needed to retain Diaz power as ruler of Mexico.

Within his Rurales group, Kosterlitzky also operated his own band of secret police and spies. These men were everywhere. They picked up all kinds of information, and they sprang from all walks of life — from the lowest peon to the highest official. His chief of spies was known as El Zorro (the Fox), who appeared to be everywhere at the same time. Yet no one knew his real identity. He might be a lowly begger one time, a drunk in a cantina another, or the owner of some shop. Suffice it to say, nobody bent on making trouble for Diaz's regime ever got away with it without Kosterlitzky knowing about it. He was kept informed of every worthwhile incident which occured in even the smallest pueblo.

Naturally, there were some people in high positions who were ambitious, and willing to start a revolution to gain their own ends. But the overthrowing of Diaz was no small matter. Most of the plots were nipped in the bud, due to Kosterlitzky and his secret police. A secret meeting might be planned by only a chosen few, yet in some mysterious manner, the Rurales leader would learn of it and send a detachment of men into the village where the secret meeting was to take place. Certain houses would be visited. The resident found himself taken before Kosterlitzky, where he would be questioned. He would speak separately to each of the accused in private. If the man could clear himself, he would be released from custody, but woe to anyone who would attempt to lie out of his predicament. Kosterlitzky had a knack for getting the truth out of a man, and the quilty man would be ordered to face a firing squad at once.

If an outlaw was captured, he would be escorted to a designated spot. There a shovel was placed in his hands and he was ordered to dig his own grave. When the grave had been dug, the doomed man would be placed at the end of it, in such a position that his body would fall into the hole. He was then shot and killed; sometimes the Rurales would fill the hole with dirt.

Many evil things have been said about Kos-terlitzky, many of them true, no doubt, but nobody could ever hint that he was a coward. Often, attempts were made on his life, yet he managed to escape every time. It appeared as though he bore a charmed life. To frustrate and humiliate anyone who tried to kill him, the colonel would enter many towns, mounted on a snow-white charger, exposing himself as a good target and defying anyone to take a shot at him.

On the contrary side of this, all would-be killers were caught and publically executed in the plaza of the pueblo. Never was an attempt made to assassinate Kosterlitzky where the assailant escaped.

One day Kosterlitzky was called to the presidential palace to confer with Diaz.

"Colonel, we must do something about this smuggling business," declared Diaz. "We are losing much revenue both ways in this matter. As an extra inducement, I am going to reward you with half of all smuggled goods you recover in breaking up these rings."

Such words were music to Kosterlitzky's ears, so he posted his Rurales to be doubly on the alert to capture these smugglers who passed goods across the international line. Not many of these men had a chance to outdo the colonel, yet there was a man named Don Jorge who did embarrass the Rurales to a great extent.

Jorge was the leader of a gang which holed up in the Sierra Madre Mountains in Sonora, from where he transported his fine Bacanora Mescal liquor into Silver City, New Mexico. In this particular case, Jorge and his men brought a good cargo across the border and exchanged it for various merchandise. Jorge knew his trip would not be hampered coming into the United States, for he realized the Rurales were not interested in his mescal, but in what he brought back. Somehow he learned that a squad of Rurales under the command of a sergeant was waiting to ambush him on his trip back to Mexico. The tricky Mexican quickly announced that he was going to hold a "baille," and would personally provide drinks for everyone who came to the dance.

The Mexicans gathered soon in huge crowds. Everyone seemed to come, all but the

44

Mexican revolutionary troops in action. These were part of Zapata's forces.

Rurales. Again, the wily Mexican acted. He called a trusted aide, gave him a flask of his strongest mescal, and told him what to do. The man, pretending he knew nothing of being watched by the Rurales, apparently sneaked the flask into the bushes and hid it. One of the Rurales picked up the potent liquor. Shortly, he and his companions were enjoying their drinks. The sergeant also appeared, took a smell of the mescal, and soon had taken his share.

Before long, every member of the Rurales squad was in deep slumber. While they slept, Don Jorge and his merry men took the trail back home. Early dawn found the Rurales hot on the trail of Jorge, but he had crossed the line to safety. During the night, Kosterlitzky and his men arrived at the line in anticipation of helping cut off the smugglers. The arrival of the sergeant and his men, without their prisoners, and still smelling of liquor, caused Colonel Kosterlitzky to fly into a rage. He slashed off the sergeant's chevrons and buttons, and reduced him to the rank of private.

There are many recorded incidents giving graphic accounts of Colonel Kosterlitzky's daring fame and penchant for justice. Here is but one of them:

In Sanuaripa lived a wealthy Castilian, whose son was wild and mean. One day the young man kidnapped the daughter of a nearby peon, took her to a distant part of his father's estate where he raped her, and then returned her to her home. The girl told her shocked parents what had happened, begging her father to compel the youth to marry her. But the father knew he was a poor, helpless peon who could not muster any strength against his wealthy neighbor.

It was the very day of the attack on the girl that Kosterlitzky rode into town with his Rurales. The father of the girl sought out the colonel, from whom he sought justice for his daughter. Kosterlitzky called in a doctor, who examined the girl, and pronounced his findings to coincide with the story told by the girl's father.

"Bring the boy and his father to me at once!" commanded the colonel to one of his aides.

Etta Place who was a noted girl friend of Butch Cassidy and the Sundance Kid was an adventurer in her own right. (See Chapter VII.) This rare photograph identifies her with Pancho Villa's troops in 1914.

When the father and his son had been brought before Kosterlitzky, he stood erect before them, a figure of power and persuasion.

"You have taken this girl against her will and made a plaything of her," he addressed the son. "Now you will marry her."

"No!" cried the father and son in one startled voice. "She's nothing but a peon, way below our station."

"Is that your final decision?"

"Yes."

Kosterlitzky motioned to several of his men. "Take these two out and place them against the adobe wall and shoot them . . . now!"

Father and son had long before heard of this Kosterlitzky, and knew he meant every word he said. They had agreed to his terms before reaching the wall. A magistrate was called, who united the young man and the peon girl in wedlock.

"And if I hear one word about any mistreatment to this girl, I'll return and finish what I set out to do," Kosterlitzky warned the two men.

This was never necessary, as the marriage proved to be a happy one, and the girl was received eventually into the wealthy family as one of its own.

When Captain Burton Mossman became commandant of the famous Arizona Rangers, he and Kosterlitzky made an agreement to cooperate with each other in handling wanted men. If a Mexican crossed into Arizona, and was captured by the Rangers, he would be turned over to Colonel Kosterlitsky, if wanted by the Rurales. If an outlaw from Arizona was wanted by Mossman and found in Mexico, Kosterlitzky would turn him over to the Rangers.

In 1906 Colonel Kosterlitzky's crack Cordado Squadron, as it was generally called, took part in quelling a riot by the miners at the Cananea Copper Mines, operated by Col. Will Greene. Most of the fighting was over, however, when he arrived, for Capt. Tom Rynning of the Arizona Rangers had crossed into Mexico with his men to try and save the lives of the Americans at the mines, but they arrived too late to do so. Yet Rynning and his three hundred miners from Brewery Gulch were able to avenge the death of the Americans by killing nearly two hundred of the strikers who fought them. Although Governor Ysabel had sworn the Americans in as willing volunteers to quell the riot, American authorities said it was an invasion of Mexico and a threat to the neutrality law. Captain Rynning narrowly missed being removed from his office.

The bloody Madero revolution broke out in Mexico in 1911, with President Porfirio Diaz being forced to flee to Spain, leaving his Rurales under the new regime. With Diaz gone, Kosterlitzky resigned, but was requested by President Francisco Madero to rejoin his Rurales, still holding the rank of colonel. Kosterlitzky cared little for Madero, and tried to keep himself from being involved in politics, but he loved Mexico, so he again took up the leadership of the Rurales. Madero requested Kosterlitzky to travel to the state of Morelos, an area controlled by the anti-Madero faction under Emiliano Zapata, supported by Pancho Villa and his outlaw band.

"Your venture would be to kill Zapata in any manner you could," Madero told him.

"Excellency," was the colonel's prompt reply. "I've killed many men, but only in honorable battle and will not stoop to assassination now. I request to be relieved of my command permanently."

President Madero shrugged.

But Colonel Kosterlitzky was not out of service for long. His successor was a poor second to the colonel, and soon law and order disappeared from the border, President Madero asked Kosterlitzky to return, and he did.

Many men who had been uncovered by Kosterlitzky for plotting against Diaz now held positions of power in the new government, and their prime interest was to dispose of the colonel and his men.

However, Madero was in office only a short time when he was assassinated, and General Victoriano Huerta set up a dictator form of government in Mexico in February 1913. Huerta was not strong enough to handle the problem. President Woodrow Wilson of the United States failed to recognize the new government and sent troops into Vera Cruz.

Mexico was in a chaotic condition. Huerta had fled the country, and insurgents of all types were roaming the land. Colonel Kosterlitzky was in command of the garrison at Nogales, Mexico when he was attacked on March 13, 1914 by a force under Col. Alvaro Obregon. With less than a thousand men, Kosterlitzky held off a superior force of nearly three thousand men. The colonel realized that after so many hours of hard fighting, his only salvation was to cross into the United States. Before doing so, however, he was determined to show his enemies how a man could really fight. Lining up his Guardia Rurales in fighting formation, he led them in one last charge. When he retreated across the international line, Colonel Kosterlitzky left a trail of blood behind him, and the streets of Nogales were covered with the bodies of his enemies.

At the end of the fight, mounted upon a magnificent white horse, Colonel Kosterlitzky crossed the line. His uniform was covered with gore, but he was still the haughty

Pancho Villa, famed revolutionary, was both feared and loved. He caused trouble on both sides of the border.

Cossack. Entering Nogales on the United States side, he rode up to the American troops.

"I wish to speak to the commanding office," he announced.

"I represent Col. Cornelius Smith," said the officer as he walked up to the colonel.

One can imagine Kosterlitzky's surprise when he saw Capt. Adna Chaffee.

"I am Col. Emilio Kosterlitzky. Here is my sword," he said, extending the blood-stained weapon to the captain.

Kosterlitzky and his men were received into the United States as refugees, and on March

Pancho Villa, Emiliano Zapata and their forces enter Mexico City triumphantly following the defeat of President Porfirio Diaz in 1911. Villa was later killed by an assassin's bullet. (See Chapter XIII.)

15 were interned at Nogales, Arizona, as prisoners of war. In October 1914, Kosterlitzky and his men were released, but the colonel and several of his officers were held by the American military authorities at Fort Rosecrans, near San Diego, California, for some unknown reason.

World attention was now focused on World War I, so it was just a formality to release Colonel Kosterlitzky. The colonel now began his further services to the United States by becoming a special employee of the Federal Bureau of Investigation. In this capacity, he continued to rule friends and enemies from Mexico, people who flocked into the United States from their homeland. He set up his own secret police system, tracing every man who arrived in Los Angeles from Mexico, until he knew every face. It was Kosterlitzky who

foiled many a counter revolution in Mexico, and placed those responsible behind prison walls, even though he never again set foot on Mexican soil after the fight at Nogales.

In later years, J. Edgar Hoover reported that Emilio Kosterlitzky was one of their finest agents, having served in the FBI from 1917 until September 1926, when he resigned due to ill health. It is fitting to state that this dynamic Cossack served the United States well indeed, from his days when he fought the dreaded Apaches in Arizona after trailing them from Mexico, until his fantastic activities in the Federal Bureau of Investigation.

On March 2, 1928, the wild Cossack passed away, still a mystery to many baffled Americans, yet to many others a name which represented courage, charm, daring, and loyalty.

Chapter Six

Henry Plummer, He Built His Own Scaffold

THE RUSTY HINGES groaned as the jail door slowly opened. Henry Plummer looked up at United States Deputy Marshal X Beidler with a sick grin.

"Funny damned thing, marshal," he said, trying hard to keep his voice steady. "I built this jail myself. The gallows, too. Never thought I'd be using them."

The marshal ignored his remark and prodded him forward. As they walked into the gray morning, Plummer said, "It's damned cold out here!"

"Don't worry, Henry," Beidler responded. "Where you're going, it'll be nice and warm!"

The date was January 10, 1864. The place was Bannack City, Montana. The populace of the boisterous gold city was up early. For them, it was an historic day. A few tears were shed, mostly by women; professional women, but no one was really sorry for Henry. He had brought about his own hanging.

At 8:00 A.M., the trap was sprung and Henry Plummer hurtled downward into eternity — on the gallows he himself had built!

Yes, as the watching townsfolk said over and over, Henry Plummer had lived mighty high off the hog. He had used his brains and gun-swift to become one of the most hated and sadistic killers the West had ever known.

Born near New Haven, Connecticut, July 6, 1832, he matured as a strikingly handsome stallion of a man, who played hell with the women from the time he was fourteen. By the time he was twenty-three, Henry had loved and labored his way clear across the continent, stopping for a time in Nevada City, California. On his second day in town, he was sunning himself on the steps of the local hotel, enlightening some drifters with tales of his mattress prowess when suddenly, he stopped mid-sentence to stare across the street. The

Courtesy Lucille M. Dixon

Henry Plummer wrote himself into history of the West with his evil deeds. He was leader of the celebrated Plummer gang which preyed on gold miners, freight trains and stagecoaches. This is believed his only known likeness. He was sheriff of two counties.

Bannack City, Montana, was the scene of wild times in the 1860s, along with Virginia City, Nevada City and Alder Gulch after gold was discovered.

object of his gaze was a lovely young woman, who had just stepped out of the general store, burdened down with packages. In answer to his unspoken question, one of the wranglers said, "Missus Vedder." He winked slyly at Plummer. "How'd you like to burn your brand onto that filly?"

Henry didn't bother to reply. In a flash he was on his feet and across the street. Ever-charming, he tipped his hat.

"How do ma'am," he said. "A pretty thing like you totin' that big bag of flour? For shame to the men of this place!"

The woman was taken aback, but readily accepted Henry's offer of assistance. As he deftly swung the fifty pound sack of flour onto the buckboard, she couldn't help but notice the stranger's good looks. And he was so charming . . .

Within minutes, they were deep in conversation. By casual questioning, Henry quickly found out all he wanted to know. The woman was young, obviously shy, but not quite so innocent. Henry couldn't help but notice her blushes. But more important, he noticed the lush, budding beauty of her figure as it swelled against the tight confines of her frontier clothes. She lived with her husband on a small ranch several miles outside of Nevada City, Henry learned, and her husband was out of town arranging for a shipment of cattle. He wasn't due back for three more days.

That evening, just after sundown, Mrs. Vedder was startled by a knock on the door of her isolated cabin. Preparing to retire early, she was already dressed in her long night garment. Clutching it tightly around her, she opened the door a crack and peered out into the night. Fearfully she asked, "Who's there?"

Who else? Freshly bathed, and dressed in clean togs, Henry Plummer placed his boot in the small opening of the door.

"Sorry to bother you ma'am, but I've had a little trouble. My horse stumbled and his leg is broken. I sure would appreciate a drink of water. I've been walking for three hours."

Quickly recognizing the charming gentleman who had so gallantly helped her that morning, Mrs. Vedder opened the door.

"Oh, I'm sorry about your horse. You must be very tired and thirsty."

Slipping a wrap about her shoulders, she led Henry behind the house to the pump, and filled the cup. He drank deeply.

"Thank you, ma'am," he said gallantly. "You're truly a lady."

As she stepped in front of him to replace the cup on the pump handle, Henry moved silently behind her. When she turned, she gasped in surprise.

"I didn't mean to frighten you," he whispered, "but you look so lovely standing there in the moonlight, your hair all long and black like that, and your skin so soft."

50

The woman caught her breath and pulled her garment more tightly about her, maybe for better concealment, maybe to accentuate the charms that Henry gazed upon with such delicate lustfulness. The Plummer charm had taken its first toll. He kissed her gently at first, and she made her token of resistance. Then slowly, the tide of passion tore her apart. She kissed him back, drinking him in with desire that had lain dormant for many weeks. Slowly, the wrap slipped from her shoulders. As Henry's practiced hands caressed her, the grip on the nightgown loosened.

Hours later, Mrs. Vedder turned softly in her sleep. Her voice made a contented sound, and she snuggled closer. Henry was awake, lying with his hands behind his head, staring satisfied into the darkness. He was deep in pleasant thought, savoring the moment, and memories of other moments and other women.

As John Vedder reined up his horse and tied it lightly at the post, Henry was oblivious. The door swung open.

"Sarah, I'm home! Sarah, are you awake?"

Sarah was awake; she had never been more awake. She was speechless with fear. As Vedder lighted the lamp, Henry's hand slid to his gun.

The room became suddenly illuminated. Vedder sucked in his breath. Then he swore loudly and went for leather. But his hand never reached the holster. Henry's sixgun went off with a roar, catching him squarely in the chest.

There was nothing they could do for the dead man on the floor, but the gun play had driven all thoughts of sleep from both their minds . . . and after all, it was still a bright moonlit night, and they were both so young Henry knew he'd probably need a friendly witness at his trial . . . and what is more friendly for two people to do?

Plummer was caught and tried for murder at Marysville. However, acting in his own defense, and supported by a friendly witness, his glib tongue spared him from the noose and he received only a light sentence. Several months later, he dramatically claimed he was dying of consumption and convinced the authorities of the truth of his claim. He was set free to die on the open prairie.

From Marysville, Henry headed to Lewis-

Fed up with outlaws, robberies and brutal killings, the miners organized a strong vigilante committee which meant business. W. F. Sanders was one of the leaders, an attorney who prosecuted outlaws and helped bring law to the wild area.

ton, Idaho. Within days, he realized that this was a town just begging to be plucked. All it needed was a man with brains, guts, and greed where his morals should have been. Henry was the man. He organized the local thugs, murderers, robbers, and easy-buck toughs, into a disciplined gang.

There wasn't the least bit of authority in Lewiston, and the Plummer gang played that advantage for all it was worth. They robbed and killed in broad daylight. Those who opposed them were murdered in cold blood. Protests mounted, but to no avail. The Plummer mob rolled forward in a wave of plunder and bloodshed.

But Henry was much too smart to take an active part. Working quietly and efficiently in the background, he remained a highly-respected member of Lewiston society. He

51

operated a faro layout and pulled the strings that kept his gunmen puppets moving. His own skill with a gun and the threat of quick death kept the gang in line. If any one had the audacity to tread on Plummer's toes, Henry would kill without batting an eyelash.

As time went by, the town became desperate. Citizens organized a vigilante committee, with the credo, "Meet gunfire with gunfire."

Henry attended the first meeting and spoke up like a preacher.

"Let me be the first man to join up," he said dramatically. "It's high time we stopped these lawless thugs."

The townspeople quickly rallied around him. The fact that he had killed several men in the streets and saloons of Lewiston was not to his discredit. Most of his victims had been ruffians and deserved to die, the other vigilantes reasoned. Henry quickly took leadership of the committee and pledged to wipe the outlaws off the face of the West. He made melodramatic speeches from street corners, urging quick justice.

But the killings went on. The robberies went on. After a time, it seemed almost suicidal to resist. The masked raiders appeared in even greater numbers, dominating the mining camps, swooping down in daylight raids, helping themselves to everything in sight, butchering all opposition.

Every plan the vigilantes made, no matter how foolproof, backfired in their faces. The outlaws knew every move they planned. They were ambushed. They were picked off in unmatched gunfights. There could be but one answer — a leak. Yet Plummer himself, the tip-off man, was never even suspected.

As the path of destruction and bloodshed widened through Lewiston, the town died. The gold fields were running dry, and quick death or robbery was the only reward for finding gold, anyway. The miners moved out finally to seek places at Elk City.

But it was the same story there, and at Florence, and everywhere else. No other bandit gang in history so dotted a state with ghost towns as did the Plummer gang. Seldom did the miners erect permanent builders; they had

grown accustomed to moving on after only a short stay in any one place.

Finally, after months of running, the miners decided to hold their ground and fight back. A life of fear and escape was not worth living. At Bannack City, Montana, they made their stand.

The town mushroomed, and wooden buildings were erected instead of temporary tents. Even the gamblers moved into wooden structures. It was a tough town — raw, wild and boisterous. Riding the crest of the boom, the people also learned to be tough. They wore their guns low. They learned to draw fast and kill first. Gradually, the tables began to turn on Henry Plummer and his gang.

Incidents increased. Slowly, but surely, the respectable facade, behind which Henry hid, crumbled. Suspicion mounted against the cultured man with the Yankee accent. Several times Henry came close to exposure. But somehow Lady Luck, plus his silvery tongue, kept him at the top of the heap. There was nothing specific or definite that could be pointed at him.

In one of his close calls, Plummer was foiled in an attempt to ambush Hank Crawford, sheriff of Bannack. Crawford, who had long held an uneasy feeling about Henry, suspected that the debonair gambler was the real leader of the territory's outlaws. Being told that Crawford was unarmed, Plummer attempted an ambush. But the tip had been incorrect. In an exchange of fire, Plummer was severely wounded in his right arm.

The shooting caused mixed feelings in Bannack. Many townspeople wished the slug had gone through Plummer's head; others were ready to lynch Crawford for the deed. But although the ambush had been unsuccessful, it accomplished Plummer's desire. Crawford knew now that his suspicions were based on fact, and that sooner or later he would fall victim to Plummer's gun. He turned in his badge and returned to his home in Wisconsin. He valued life too highly to wait around for inevitable death.

Plummer recovered from the wound, but his gun arm was useless. He practiced day and night, until he could draw and fan off shots

The vigilantes had many of the outlaws spotted by their necktie knots and handshakes. When the cleanup began, five were hanged in January 1864 from a beam in this partly-completed store building in the center of Virginia City. Plummer was unsuspected at first. The building still stands and rope scars are seen by tourists.

expertly with his left hand. He knew that if his secret got out, one of his own men would probably gun him down, but during practicing sessions, he had to entrust the gang's leadership to one of his more deadly gunfighters, Boone Helm.

Helm was a depraved killer, a man with a lurid past. From the time he was old enough to wield a gun, he had not hesitated to kill. A story was circulated in Bannack that in his younger days, Helm had once participated in cannibalism during a snow-bound siege in the Snake River Country. This was the man in whom Plummer placed his trust. This was the type of filth which comprised the Plummer gang.

Helm was a native of Log Branch, Missouri, near the home of the James brothers, and had committed his first murder when still a lad by stabbing a young friend to death. He fled

to Salt Lake City, Utah, where he became a hired killer for awhile, but where again, he was forced to flee.

At Florence, Idaho, he shot down an unarmed man, but he bribed the jailer and escaped as the gallows were being erected. In San Francisco he lived high, throwing gold about recklessly until he murdered a man in a fight over a woman, and had to run once again. He was known, then, in Oregon, where he was branded a cannibal.

Hired as a guide for six men trekking from the Grand Ronde Valley, Oregon, to Salt Lake City, he started the trip in the dead of winter. Within a few weeks, ripped by blizzards and stinging rain, the group played out, until one day only Helm and E. Burton survided. Burton cracked after their provisions ran out when they were trapped in the frozen wilderness. He committed suicide in the Snake River

53

Country in Idaho. Helm butchered Burton's body as he would that of a steer, and carried the legs of the luckless traveler in a bag slung over his shoulder, until he staggered into a Blackfoot Indian along the trail.

Henry learned to used his left hand with deadly accuracy, and before long he re-took full leadership of the gang. The band grew even stronger, and was soon able to swing considerable political pressure.

The first man to test Henry's new skill was an old-time cronie named Jack Cleveland. He had come to town and had demanded a cut in the Plummer operations. He knew what was going on, for he was well-acquainted with Plummer from years back when they were partners-in-crime. Henry ignored the man's demands. On January 14, 1863, Cleveland and Plummer shot it out in Goodrich's saloon in Bannack.

"Damn you, Plummer!" cried Cleveland. "I'll get you now, and that will wind you up for good!"

But Henry had other ideas. Apparently Cleveland believed his gun hand was faster than Plummer's, for with lightning speed his right hand streaked toward his holster. He was a split second too late. Henry's hand had darted downward with the uncanny speed of a hissing cobra. His gun leveled and triggered before Cleveland knew what was happening. Plummer's heavy slug slammed his victim back against the bar, and he slumped to the saw-dust-covered floor in a limp heap, mortally wounded.

Most of the people there believed Cleveland to be a member of the ghost-like gang of bandits, and no citizen offered to help him, so great was their fear of the outlaw band. Cleveland lived for several hours after someone had volunteered to carry him to his room. Henry remained with Cleveland until the dying man asked him to get him a blanket. Plummer did not wish to leave the room for fear of what Cleveland might say. When Henry returned, the man was dead.

The Goodrich Hotel, Montana's first hostelry, and Skinner's Saloon next door were scenes of many fights and gun battles. Henry Plummer held full reign in the town which was also the first capital.

No one was around except several miners.

"Did he say anything?" asked Plummer.

"About what?" one asked curiously.

"Oh, about his family, his past life, anyone to notify?"

"Cleveland had no friends," said another old-timer. "I will see he is buried, though; that's the least one man can do for another, no matter what."

"Suit yourself," said Plummer, leaving the room.

Later, one evening, the suave gunman leaped on top of the faro table at the local saloon and announced to the startled drinkers that he was going to run for sheriff in the departed Crawford's place. When he finished his brazen speech, he asked, "Any objections?"

There were none.

The election was an outrage, for Plummer's true colors were now known to most of the miners. Yet his outlaw band swung enough weight to elect him sheriff.

As soon as he had pinned on the badge, the tough but helpless citizens were ready to leave Bannack, for terror and death became the order of the day. But Plummer's reign was short-lived, anyway, for a sensational gold strike by Bill Fairweather at Alder Gulch, Montana, sent the miners scampering.

Plummer was left ruling a ghost town, so he packed up and moved to Virginia City, Montana, a boisterous place of gold, gunsmoke, and bawdy houses.

William Fairweather was a strange man who knew no fear, nor did he care for or greatly value gold. He would ride up and down the street of Virginia City, scattering gold dust right and left in the street to see the children and Chinese laborers scramble for it. What he did not throw away, he drank up. He died at the age of 39, in 1875, and was buried on a hill overlooking the stream that gave millions in gold to the world. There is an iron fence around the grave with a gold plate inscribed: "William H. Fairweather, captain of party who discovered Alder Gulch, May, 1863. Born in Woodstock Parish, Carlton County, New Brunswick, June 14th, 1836. Died, 1875, at Daly's Ranch, Madison County, Montana, August 25th."

Most of the population of Virginia City was too busy getting rich to worry about civic affairs, so Henry Plummer got at tight grip on the votes of the boomtown, threw off his guise as a gambler, and became a full-time gang chief. His more respectable-looking hoodlums were appointed judges, deputies, and clerks. Boone Helm became the leader of the deputies, and once again, Henry was the power behind the scenes. The money rolled in through fines assessed on order of Plummer to the judges, and his men, in the guise of clerks, worked in every business place in town.

More open than ever in his threats and blackmailing activities, Henry Plummer tried to get the choicest plum of them all — an appointment as United States Deputy Marshal. But here, the lawman Nathaniel Langford dared to testify against his character, and Plummer did not win the coveted appointment.

The lack of mail service between Virginia City and the nearest express office at Salt Lake City, five hundred miles away, gave Plummer his best opportunity to steal. Money had to be carried across the country by private messenger, and Plummer controlled a clerk in almost every office where the money was handled.

There was a stage line between Virginia City and the once roaring Bannack, which was now but an intermediary post. At each end of the line, Plummer had agents keeping him supplied with information on shipments of gold. Gunmen ravaged the line, their smoking weapons dealing death to anyone who resisted them. When the stages carried anything worth stealing, a Plummer agent marked the stage with a secret symbol. Other agents noted the identifying mark and passed the word along. In the hills, Plummer's raiders waited in their hideouts, and when a messenger dashed in with the tip-off, masked riders swept down on route, killed or threatened passengers, and stole everything of value.

The Plummer men wore only mustaches and side-whiskers, which were somewhat out-of-fashion in this era of full beards. They had a special handclasp and used the password "innocent" as further identification.

Boot Hill at Virginia City contains graves of outlaws who were given a quick drop to enternity by vigilantes in January 1864. A similar spot is on a hill above Bannack. Tourists today visit the locations by stagecoach and car.

Plummer was sheriff of Virginia City and Bannack at the same time. Whenever he received word of a holdup, he canvassed the saloons and dives, gathered a heavily armed posse, and gave chase dramatically . . . but he never caught any of the bandits. Once a driver eagerly told the posse he could make positive identification of the killers if he ever saw them again.

"You sure you'll know these men when you see them?" Plummer asked.

"Certain."

"You come with me," Plummer told the driver.

"Sure thing, it will be a good thing to get some of these outlaws out of the way," said the proud driver. "I'm anxious to be of help."

Plummer and the driver rode out of earshot of the remainder of the posse.

"Guess you want to keep this confidential between us, eh, sheriff? grinned the stage driver.

"That is correct. But you made a bad mistake by talking too much."

Plummer drew swiftly and blasted the unsuspecting driver from his saddle. Then he fired several more shots into the hills, and removing his coat, fired another bullet through the sleeve. When the posse converged on the spot, they found Plummer standing beside the dead man.

"They ambushed as he came over that rise," he told the men. "One bullet nicked my coat," and he pointed to the hole in his sleeve. "A couple of them headed south."

He mounted his horse and, leaving a man beside the murdered driver, led the posse off on a wild-goose chase across the hills.

Others who believed they could identify the robbers died under strange circumstances. Incredibly, even Plummer's bitterest enemies still failed to realize he was the man who was calling every shot for the outlaws.

But his luck was running out. Suspicion was first confirmed in the minds of his enemies when he himself held up a young miner named Tilden who was carrying a considerable amount of gold . . . too much for Plummer to be able to resist. Returning to town, Tilden sought out several friends.

"Damned if that masked man didn't look uncommon like Hank Plummer," he told them.

A few days later, Plummer received word that a party was leaving Virginia City with a heavy load of gold. He sent out two of his deadliest deputies, Dutch John Wagner and Steve Marshland, to intercept the party.

"Wipe them out!" Plummer commanded.

This time, as the gold train drove past, Dutch John squeezed off a shot and missed. Warned, the riders whirled their horses and jumped for cover, dragging their pack mules into the brush. The peaceful afternoon came alive with a burst of gunfire. Dutch John fell first, then Marshland was knocked flat with a slug. The two gunfighters dragged themselves to their horses and made their getaway, but not before they had been recognized.

News of the attack by two of Plummer's deputies spread through the mining camp.

"Plummer's at the bottom of this trouble!" they cried.

People recalled quickly that one of Plummer's men, George Ives, had been hanged at Nevada City on December 21, 1863, for the murder of a young miner named Nick Tbalt near Alder Gulch, the area of the great gold strikes.

"Plummer was responsible for Tbalt's death!" went the excited talk. "Plummer did this, too."

The anti-Plummer faction leaped upon the rumors, fired the entire town with the zeal to get Plummer — to give him what he deserved. This led to the formation of the Montana Vigilantes, which eventually cleaned up the area and got rid of all the outlaws. However, this group was not officially formed until after the hanging of Plummer.

Two sister towns, Virginia and Nevada, claimed the honor of taking the first steps toward the formation of a vigilante committee.

As a matter of fact, five men in Virginia and one in Nevada commenced at the same time to take the initiative in this matter. Two days had not elapsed before their efforts were united, and the ramifications of the league of safety and order extended in a week or two all over the territory. On January 14, 1864, the *coup de grace* was given to the power of the law-and-order group by the execution of five of the chief villains in Virginia City.

On January 4, 1864, two thousand armed miners stormed through the streets of Bannack. Fortunately for Plummer he was out of town, but two of his deputies, Erastus "Red" Yeager and G. W. Brown, were caught near Stinkingwater Valley.

"Hank Plummer is sheriff around here," these deputies protested," and we're his assistants. We're the only legal peace officers in the territory. You got no authority for hanging us or trying."

The kill-crazed mob hauled Yeager and Brown to the nearest tree to hang them without trial or ceremony. Begging for mercy, Red Yeager confessed to several murders, and reeled off the names of a dozen Plummer gunmen who had worn badges.

"Plummer's the leader!" cried Yeager. "He's the one you want!"

But the doomed men's protests did no good. They threw a noose around Yeager's neck and

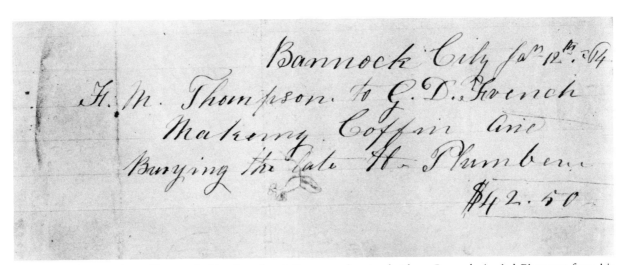

When tipped as to Henry Plummer's identity, the vigilantes made a hard ride to Bannack, hauled Plummer from his bed, and quickly hanged him. In a last letter to his wife, Plummer tried to blame his actions on the Civil War and loyalty to the Union. This (above) was the order for his coffin, which cost $42.50.

hauled him off the ground. He struggled and jerked like a puppet at the end of a string. Brown was next. The date was January 4, 1864, just ten days before the Montana Vigilantes came into being.

The crowd next turned its attention toward the remaining outlaw deputies. Several of them had fled when the mob first gathered, but others were trapped in the raging town. Volley after volley of heavy bullets were fired through the town in such a haphazard manner that it was a wonder half the citizens were not killed. Screams of panic-stricken children and terrified women intermingled with the pitiful neighing of horses struck by bullets.

When the final curtain of smoke was laid some time later, most of the Plummer gang had been disposed of.

The men bent on restoring law and order in Montana went to Plummer's home in Bannack, dragged him from his bed, and placed him in his own jail. Deputies Buck Stinson and Ned Ray, who were also in town, were captured and hanged immediately.

Plummer wrote to his wife, "This territory has been taken over by Confederate bushwhackers, and, although I'm the duly elected sheriff, I'm about to be lynched because of my loyalty to the Union."

That was a classic example of Henry's gall!

Plummer was only thirty-two years of age, and his crime career had lasted only a few years, but they were bloody years for Montana. He himself had killed fifteen men, and his subordinates had committed more than a hundred murders at his command.

Sitting there waiting for Beidler to swing open the cell gate and lead him to the scaffold, Plummer probably reflected on those wasted years. Had he used his brains in legitimate fields, he might well have prospered. Plummer had a keen mind and a fine appearance. He had successfully operated several bakeries in Nevada City, and doubtless had the energy and imagination to have explored the rich mining possibilities of the time and place, had he chosen to do so. But once he tasted the power and the comfort of the rich outlaw's life, it was impossible for him to turn back.

"Get going," Beidler said. He twisted the key in the lock and pulled open the iron door.

Plummer walked through and looked around.

"Damnedest thing," he muttered. "I'm the one that built this jail."

"Yes, and the scaffold as well," Beidler agreed.

Out in the bright morning the crowd of miners he had victimized stood waiting. Inside a nearby building sat men who had known Plummer personally, and did not want to face him on this upsetting occasion. Also nearby, in another structure, the men who were forming the vigilantes made further plans, meanwhile keeping a watchful eye on the proceedings.

Plummer mounted the scaffold. Then his nerve cracked. As he stared through the loop, tears streamed from his eyes, and he began to beg.

"Don't hang me. For God's sake, don't hang me!" he cried, dropping to his knees.

"My wife in Connecticut knows nothing of this. Give me another chance."

Beidler hauled him to his feet and slipped the noose again around Henry's neck. The struggling man plunged through the trap, his falling body becoming sharply arrested at the end of the rope, and a sharp crack echoed through Bannack's streets, writing an end to Plummer's outlaw career.

On January 14, 1864, just four days after Plummer was executed, Boone Helm was arrested while trying to flee the area. Vainly he protested against the charges hurled at him, but they just laughed in his face. His fate was immediate hanging in Virginia City.

Calmly Helm cracked jokes as he was led to the box scaffold. He was not afraid to die, and stood coolly to the end. As he stepped up on the box, he turned and bellowed his last defiant words worthy of a vastly better man.

"Every man for his principle! Hurrah for Jeff Davis! Let 'er rip!"

The executioner jerked the box from under his feet, and into eternity went one of the vilest of Plummer's aides.

The very last of the Plummer gang to die was Bill Hunter. He tried to escape the terri-

Henry Plummer wound up in a wind-swept grave on a small hillside back of Bannack. The grave is visible at lower left. Members of his gang are buried nearby.

tory and managed to get as far as Milk Creek Ranch when he was hemmed in by a giant snowstorm. Before he was able to continue his flight, four vigilantes arrived at the ranch and captured him while he slept there before the fireplace. He was promptly hanged.

Several months later, Plummer's young wife visited in Virginia City and in Bannack. She interviewed miners and leafed through the scanty records, seeking some confirmation that her husband had been lynched by Confederate sympathizers, as he had written her. People liked her, and were sympathetic to her quest.

Many people were beginning to think the hanging of Henry Plummer might have been a mistake. But finally, even his wife admitted her husband had been a blackguard and that his execution had been just.

The people were kind to Mrs. Plummer and afforded her every comfort, well-knowing she had nothing to do with her husband's depravity. History, too, has been kind to her, for no account has been kept of her movements. She dropped completely from sight after her tragic visit to Montana.

Chapter Seven

Butch Cassidy and the Raiders of Robbers Roost

ALTHOUGH THERE IS some controversy as to where "Butch" Cassidy, whose real name was Robert Leroy Parker, was born, it is an established fact that the family Bible recording shows the place as Circle Valley, April 6, 1866, some miles north of Circleville, Utah.

Robert Parker spent his early life just as any other rancher's young son might do. He learned to ride and became an expert horseman, as well as learning the art of handling and using various firearms. One day his father hired a young man named Mike Cassidy to work on his spread. Parker was captivated by the young outlaw, and Cassidy soon learned he had another admirer as well as a possible owl-hoot follower.

Mike Cassidy taught Parker all the tricks of rapid fire and fast draw. He showed him many things that would benefit an outlaw on the trail and in need of protection. One day Cassidy said to Parker, "Kid, I've got to go to Mexico, saddle up my horse, pronto."

That was the last Robert Leroy Parker ever saw of his idol, outlaw Mike Cassidy. So much had this man impressed the youth that when he left his father's ranch soon after, he did so using the name of George Cassidy.

On November 3, 1887, a Denver & Rio Grande train was stopped and held up by four men near Grand Junction, Colorado. No money was obtained because the express clerk refused to deliver up the key to the safe. The four robbers decided to abandon the job and

not to kill the young messenger for his brazen nerve. It has been said by various authors that Cassidy (Parker) was a member of this band, but this is doubtful. It is believed that the two notorious McCarty brothers were present, as well as Ed Rhodes and Bob Boyle. The sheriff of Gunnison, Colorado, who captured several of the outlaws, never placed Cassidy among them.

Cassidy graduated from petty thievery and horse stealing to bank robbery in 1880. In Mancos, Colorado, he met Matt Warner, the black sheep of a Mormon bishop family named Christiansen, and Tom McCarty, Matt's brother-in-law. On June 24, the three of them invaded the San Miguel Bank at Telluride, Colorado, and robbed it of about $11,000 in cash.

The outlaws, after a touch-and-go race with a determined posse, reached the safe confines of Brown's Hole, an area where lawmen did not relish entering. Tom and Matt went on to Star Valley, where Warner bought a saloon with his share of the bank loot. His place soon became the headquarters for members of all the local gangs. For wallpaper, the place was decked with banknotes which were of no value to the gangs, for one reason or another.

Cassidy rode on to Lander, Wyoming, where he teamed up with a young cowhand named Al Hainer, and they established the Wind River horse ranch. It was not long before they had acquired a nice band of horses, which they rode into old Lander, and disposed of the animals to a horse dealer. With the proceeds from the sale, the two "ranchers" did up the place; before long, their bank roll had disappeared in that wild, wide-open cowtown.

Hainer and Cassidy always managed to return to Lander with a pocketful of money. No embarrassing questions were asked; they were well-supplied with cash, and that was what counted. The next time the pair came into town, they were accompanied by officers of the law, charged with rustling. When brought to trial, Al Hainer was acquitted, but Cassidy, on July 3, 1894, was convicted of resisting arrest rather than the rustling charge, and was sentenced to serve two years in the Wyoming State Prison.

Following his conviction, Cassidy was taken from Fremont County to the state prison at Laramie, where, on July 15, he entered the gates as convict No. 187. He was twenty-eight years old, five-feet-eleven-inches tall, with light complexion, blue eyes, chestnut hair, and place of birth given as New York city, under the name of Butch Cassidy. As the prisoner had relatives living in Sevier Valley and in Circleville, Utah, he chose to give his alias and a fake birthplace. He was using the name "Butch," as this nickname had been given to him while he had worked in a butchershop in Rock Springs, Wyoming, in 1892.

Butch managed to maintain a good record at the prison. After serving nineteen months, he requested a pardon of Governor William A. Richards. It was granted. On the day Butch left the prison, January 16, 1896, the governor said to him "Butch, will you give me your word to go straight?"

Butch thought for a few moments. "Governor, that I cannot do; I do not want to break my word with you."

"All right, then, will you promise not to molest any bank or commit any other crime in the state of Wyoming?"

This Butch Cassidy agreed to do.

Young Cassidy had entered the prison a tossel-headed, devil-may-care, smiling cowhand, and to all outward appearances, remained that same smiling individual. Yet, beneath it all there lies the frustration of a wrong inflicted upon him. "Given the name, he would play the game." The result was one of the most adroit robbers in the history of

This rare shot of Butch Cassidy astride his horse was taken in 1912 at Juarez. Cassidy was everywhere in the West and likely took part in the revolt below the border, for he was always the adventurer.

BUTCH CASSIDY
Juarez - 1912

Matt Warner, whose real name was Christensen, was a member of the Butch Cassidy gang. He was arrested and tried in 1896, spending time in the Utah State Pentitentiary.

the West. Yet, in all of his career, he never established a record as a killer, and never was he accused of murder. David C. Thornhill, a leading Pinkerton agent of the time, said this: "Butch was not the type to make a real bad man. He was too 'soft-hearted' to ever become a killer."

This was fantastic indeed, that a man who surrounded himself with some of the most vicious and homicidal outlaws, and over whom he exercised complete domination, should be able to establish such a record. Butch, at times of necessity, was compelled to use his gun to save himself, but at such times, he simply would wound his man enough to put him out of commission.

Upon his release from prison, Butch made his way back to Brown's Hole. In May 1896, Matt Warner was involved in the hired killing of several miners on Dry Ford Creek. Matt was in desperate need of money, so he and Cassidy rode to Montpelier, Idaho, where they robbed the bank of some five thousand dollars. Some reports have claimed that Cassidy, Bob Meeks, and Elza Lay robbed this bank on August 13, 1896.

Shortly thereafter, Matt Warner was arrested and accused of murdering two miners named Melton and Staunton at Dry Forks, Utah. Matt had sold his saloon and moved to Ogden, Utah, where he married. To assist Matt's case, Cassidy hired four well-known criminal lawyers to defend him. They were D. N. Straup, F. L. Luther, Judge Powers, and John Preston. The defense was brilliant, but no match for the testimony of several eyewitnesses to the murders. Matt was convicted and sentenced to the Utah State Penitentiary.

Butch Cassidy returned again to Brown's Hole, more than ever a hero to his men. Butch had wanted to try a bold stroke in an effort to liberate Matt Warner from jail, but Matt wrote him a note, telling him not to do it.

In 1897 Butch and his men drifted down to Price, Utah, where they learned the date the miners of the Castle Gate Pleasant Valley Coal Company were to be paid. On April 21st, Butch Cassidy, Bob Meeks, and Elza Lay rode into Castle Gate. About 1:00 P.M., they held up the paymaster as he was carrying about nine thousand dollars to cover the mine payroll. This, along with a herd of cattle rustled on their way through Colorado, set up the gang on easy street for awhile. They holed up in Ladore Canyon until the excitement was over; then they headed for Baggs and the town of Dixon, on the Little Snake River.

The band consisted of the following men, at one time or another: Flat-Nose George Curry, Utah killer; Bob Lee, alias Curry, cousin of Harvey Logan; Merino Kid; Bill Ray; Ike Maxwell; Monte Butler; Lew McCarthy; Jack Peterson; Morry Kofford; Bob Meeks; Joe Marigarin; Lew Johnson; Camella Hanks; Albert Bender; Joe Walker; Bob Culp, killed near Price; George Leigh; Tom Thompson; Jim Lamb, and Elza Lay, alias Bob McGinnis. Others were Buzzard Bennett, Tom King, Tracy (not Harry), and Lamb, all hanged by a mob, and Steve Megger, hanged at Vernal, Utah. Then there was Matt Warner, of course, who went to prison and who lived until December 19, 1938, passing away at the age of 74. He had been released from prison and was a model citizen thereafter, even becoming a peace officer.

There were other members too, but old-timers at the game. Teton Jackson, outlaw from Jackson Hole, at times was with the gang. He was a college man and came from a fine family of New England. Teton, it is claimed, belonged to Brigham Young's "destroying angels," and was known as the "Messenger of the Mormons." He was captured by United States Marshal Frank M. Canton, served his time, and reformed.

Harvey Logan, alias "Kid Curry," was the real tiger of the Wild Bunch, and mean as they come. Pinkerton Agent Thornhill claims that Harvey Logan committed suicide when surrounded by a posse near Rifle, Colorado, after the holdup of the train near Parachute on June 7, 1904. However, some claimed that the body of the dead man was that of Jim York, even though the Pinkerton Detective Agency men identified it as that of Kid Curry. Detective Lowell Spence identified the body, which was buried in "Potters Field" in Glenwood Springs, Colorado.

In 1911, a man suffering from pneumonia was admitted to the Denver State Hospital and gave his name as Harvey Logan. Friends identified the man as Logan. Another report,

and probably the most logical one, stated that Logan died in Patagonia, South America, in 1909, after being fatally kicked by a mule. He did admit that he had participated in the "Parachute robbery," going to South America a year after. It might be added that none of the thirty thousand dollars reward money offered for the capture or death of Kid Curry was ever paid!

Bill Carver, Ben Kilpatrick, Harvey Logan, and Harry Longabaugh, the Sundance Kid, had been members of the Black Jack Ketchum gang, prior to joining the Cassidy Wild Bunch.

In 1898 part of the so-called Butch Cassidy gang staged a raid upon the cattle range near Price, Utah, but fell afoul of the law, and a number of the outlaws were killed or captured. Among the slain was one man thought to be the outlaw leader, but when the body was identified by the sheriff, who knew Butch well, they discovered the dead rustler was Bob Culp, who in many ways resembled Butch Cassidy.

The outbreak of the Spanish-American War filled most of the outlaws with an urge to participate. They sent letters to the governors of Utah, Colorado, and Wyoming, stating they would serve in the Second United States Cavalry, then being organized as "Teddy's Rough Riders," if they would be granted am-

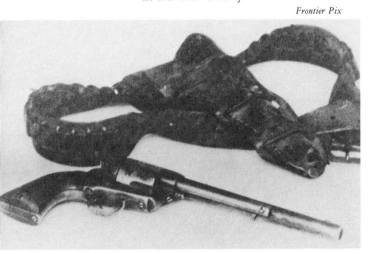

Matt Warner carried this gun and holster, perhaps when he ran with Cassidy.

Frontier Pix

Later, Matt Warner became a "good guy" and even a deputy sheriff. This was his badge, donated to collector by his daughter, Joyce.

Courtesy Ron Donoboh

"Black Jack" Ketchum was leader of a notorious robber band in the West, often using Cassidy gang members for backup. He was captured and hanged in New Mexico in 1901.

ing one of his trips hunting mountain lions, had run into this almost inaccessible location, and while hunting some stray horses, he met Butch on Yellow Creek in western Colorado. Wells was never molested by any of the Long Riders.

Early on the morning of June 2, 1899, part of the gang, probably the Currys and Elza Lay, held up and robbed the Union Pacific train at Wilcox, Wyoming, of over sixty thousand dollars in unsigned bank notes.

On Saturday following the robbery, a special Union Pacific train arrived at Casper with men and horses in charge of Sheriff Hazen of Converse County. Following the outlaws out of an area around Salt Creek, Sheriff Hazen was shot and killed from ambush by Kid Curry. This action caused a hue and cry across the state; it was dangerous for the outlaws to be seen by anyone. Upon reaching the Little Muddy, near Fort Washakie, the loot was divided and the gang scattered.

Back in 1896, Butch Cassidy could muster some fifty followers, but at the turn of the century, times had changed. The states of Utah, Colorado, Wyoming, Arizona, and Idaho, all enraged at the depredations of the various gangs of outlaws, were determined to exterminate them. Butch Cassidy saw the handwriting on the wall. In 1900 he was planning on a change of climate, building up a reserve fund, and taking off for South America.

On the evening of August 29, 1900, the Union Pacific train passed the Tipton, Wyoming, station, and approached Table Rock. As the train slowed down on an upgrade, the engineer found himself suddenly staring into the barrel of a wicked-looking .45. Kid Curry ordered the conductor, E. J. Kerrigan, to uncouple all the cars but the express and mail cars, which were right behind the engine. After the train had moved up the track for several miles, minus the passenger cars and the caboose, the robbers demanded that the express car doors be opened. At first, the order was refused, but upon the threat of being dynamited in the car, the clerk at last opened the doors. Three charges of dynamite broke open the safe, which contained a little over five thousand dollars.

nesty. This proposition was turned down as there were too many serious charges against the outlaws to justify such action.

The late Billy Wells, for whom Wells, Wyoming, was named, ran a ranch, but his principal occupation was that of a hunter and guide for wealthy sportsmen. From 1890 until 1910, he established several hunting lodges with supplies of camp equipment, hounds, and guides. Billy was a pioneer in what today is called a "dude rancher." According to him, it was he who told Butch Cassidy about the canyon country, where the outlaw later established his famous "Robbers Roost." Wells, dur-

64

The robbers involved in the action at Tipton probably were Kid Curry, Bill Carver, Camella Hanks, and several others, unknown. It has been said that Butch Cassidy was also present, but his name was never connected openly with this robbery.

On July 11, 1899, "Black Jack" Ketchum, his brother, Sam, Elza Lay, Kid Curry, and Camella Hanks held up the Colorado and Southern train near Folsom, eighty miles south of Trinidad, Colorado. Sam was wounded and later died, on July 24. Elza Lay was wounded twice, captured, and sent to the state penitentiary. His real name was William Ellsworth Lay, born November 25, 1871, in McArthur, Vinton County, Ohio. He was later released and spent the remainder of his life as a good citizen, dying November 10, 1934, and was buried in Forest Lawn Memorial Park, Glendale, California.

Tom "Black Jack" Ketchum tried to hold up the same train on August 16. He was shot in the attempt, captured, tried, convicted, and hanged at Clayton, New Mexico. All this time, Butch was at the ranch of the Taylor family, near Vernal, taking off only once to help rob the Castle Gate paymaster.

On September 19, 1900, Butch Cassidy, Harry Longabaugh (the Sundance Kid), Ben Kilpatrick (the Tall Texan), and Harvey Logan rode into Winnemucca, Nevada. It was around noon. Tying their horses to the hitch rack, the four walked into the First National Bank. They appeared shortly on the wooden sidewalk, richer by $32,650.

Edward A. Ducker, a member of the posse which was organized, was studying law in the office of C. D. Van Duzer, about a block west of the bank, when gunfire brought him and other citizens into the street. In front of the bank building, Mr. Nixon, president of the First National, and a man named Johnson, were yelling that the bank had been robbed. A mad rush was started to secure horses to follow the bandits, who were last seen crossing the bridge spanning the Humboldt River.

Deputy Sheriff George Rose commandeered an engine to overtake the fleeing robbers. Although the tracks paralleled the road taken by the outlaws, a distance of five hundred feet separated the engine from the raiders. The distance, as well as the jolting engine, prevented the officers from scoring any hits. The engine returned to town after the rails turned away from the road.

About six miles from Winnemucca, the mounted posse discovered the spot where the outlaws had camped the previous night. It was also at that spot that Butch Cassidy compelled Bill Carver to await their return from town. Bill was such a homicidal maniac that the outlaw leader decided to leave him out of the robbery for fear he would kill someone. At this camp, Carver had waited with fresh horses. As the bandits crossed the river, the lawmen saw their quarry far across the sagebrush flats, headed east toward Ruby Range. The pursuit was abandoned at that point. Some years ago, this author took a ride over the same trail used by the bandits in fleeing from town. It was quite an experience. The route ran as follows:

By-passing old Goldcona, Battle Mountain and Dumphy, then going between Elko, Carlin, and Palaside, and across the flats into Lamolle Valley; then into the foothills which led into Secret Pass, which leads across the Ruby Range into Polo Canyon and Clover Valley.

Reaching Clover Valley, the outlaws headed north and arrived at Suers' Ranch. Butch was

Frontier Pix

This pistol belonged to robber-highwayman "Black Jack" Ketchum.

65

Butch Cassidy's key members of his gang dressed in their best and boldly posed for this classic photo in Fort Worth, Texas. The photographer placed a copy in his window where a Pinkerton agent recognized some of the bandits. The detective had many copies made for wide distribution. Shown are, from left, top row: Bill Carver, Harvey Logan; below, Harry Longabaugh (Sundance Kid), Ben Kilpatrick, Butch Cassidy.

a methodical man and left little to chance. A week prior to the holdup he had stopped at this ranch, leading a string of horses, and stating that he was a horse and cattle buyer going into White Pine County to purchase stock. He requested and received permission to leave the extra stock until his return.

Now, after the robbery, he was far ahead of the posse, so he stopped at Suers place for their fresh mounts. Here, they procured the horses left in the man's charge and continued riding, leading the fresh animals along. After these animals had warmed up, the bandits could switch to them and still easily outdistance the posse. Several officers did follow the trail as far as the south Idaho line, where it petered out, and then returned to Winnemucca, as had the larger portion of the posse.

The outlaws made their way to Fort Worth, Texas, where they met Kid Curry. One fine day, with several drinks under their belts, they decided to have their pictures taken. Dressed in their Sunday best, the five desperadoes strolled calmly into Schwartz's Photograph Gallery on November 21, 1900, where they posed for pictures. The gang ordered a number of copies, paying for them in advance, and asked they be delivered to Fannie Porter's place. It was at Fannie's that the Sundance Kid again saw Etta Place. Probably it was the first time he had seen her since they were children back in Pennsylvania. She was not one of Fannie's call girls, but more of an aide to Fannie in other ways.

It might be well to mention here that Longabaugh married Annie Marie Thayn in the summer of 1900, and she gave birth to his son in February 1901. At that time, the Sundance Kid and Etta Place were on their way to South America. There is also evidence that Etta Place gave birth to two daughters in South America, both probably Cassidy's children. There is little doubt that Cassidy and Etta were lovers, but more than this, probably man and wife.

Photographer Schwartz, impressed by the liberal actions of his five customers, wanted to do them a favor too, so he placed a copy of the picture in his display gallery. One day Fred Dodge, a Pinkerton agent, passed the photo shop and glanced at the picture. Then he halted, taking another good look. He recognized Bill Carver as a long-wanted man; the others in the group he was unable to identify. He secured the photo from Mr. Schwartz and took it to police headquarters, where all five men were identified as wanted men. Dodge ordered copies of the photo by the gross. These were quickly distributed throughout the country. Butch and his right hand bower, Harry Longabaugh, went into hiding, while Bill Carver, Ben Kilpatrick, and Harvey Logan went to visit the Carver home near Bandera, Texas.

Shortly thereafter, the trio traveled to the Kilpatrick ranch, located between Eden and Paint Rock, in Concho County, Texas. However, the inactivity proved irksome, so Carver, Kilpatrick, and Logan, accompanied by Ben's brother George, decided to visit Eden. When the boys arrived in town, they were spotted by Oliver Thornton, a rancher who lived near Eden, and who knew Bill Carver well. Carver, fearing that Thornton would betray them to the law, drew his revolver and killed the rancher. An irate posse pursued the outlaws, but they made good their getaway.

The outlaws headed for Sonora, Texas, where they camped at the edge of town. Bill Carver and George Kilpatrick rode into town for supplies. While purchasing foodstuffs and the like, they aroused the suspicions of Sheriff E. J. Bryant, who followed them with a deputy when the outlaws left town. Carver did not like this idea, so he turned and fired on the officers. Bryant was not caught napping. When the firing ceased, Bill Carver was dead and George Kilpatrick was seriously wounded. Later, he recovered and was released, since he had never been a part of the gang, and there was no wanted record on him. Back at camp,

This photograph was staged by M. J. Monette (right rear), co-owner of the famed Mohawk Mine at Goldfield, Nevada. He wished to dramatize the mine's great richness and hired two well-known guards. The one on the left is believed to be Butch Cassidy.

Ben Kilpatrick and Harvey Logan heard the gunfire and knew what it meant. They quickly fled the vicinity . . . it was April 2, 1901.

In February 1901 two men and a beautiful woman stopped at the boardinghouse of Mrs. Thompson at 325 East 14th Street, New York City. Anyone who knew the trio would have recognized them as Butch Cassidy, Harry Longabaugh, and Etta Place. What such desperate men were doing in New York City was certainly a puzzle. We know they took in the sights for several weeks. They also had their pictures taken at the De Young Portrait Studios at 826 Broadway. One day a coded wire came to the hotel where James Ryan (Butch Cassidy) was staying. It was from Kid Curry.

"Sundance, you and Etta go to South America. I'll see you there sometime this year yet. I've got a chore to do with Logan."

So it was. Butch returned to his old haunts to participate in one more robbery, although some sources claim he did not. It still is a moot question. The Sundance Kid and Etta Place boarded the steamship S. S. *Soldier Prince* under the names of Mr. and Mrs. Harry D. Place, bound for Buenos Aires, Argentina.

There are existing records stating that the outlaws in this raid on July 3, 1901, upon the Great Northern Railroad, were Butch Cassidy, Kid Curry, Ben Kilpatrick and his girl friend, Laura Bullion. Reports from crewmen who were present said only three men were seen, no woman. Of course, Butch could have remained in the background, as did Camella Hanks, who was holding the getaway horses.

On that fateful day of July, the Oriental Limited, crack train of the Great Northern, stopped at Malta, Montana, to refuel and take on water. As the train pulled out of Malta, Kid Curry boarded the baggage car right behind the coal tender. Five miles this side of Wagner, he crawled into the engine and covered the fireman and engineer with his .45s. Curry ordered engineer Thomas Jones to throw the brakes, then to uncouple the express car and pull the engine and car down the tracks.

Half a mile from the split train, the engine was halted again, and the crew escorted back to the express car. They were ordered to instruct the express messenger to open up. The brave but foolhardy man refused to comply.

"We're going to blow up the car and you with it," warned Kid Curry.

The messenger quickly opened the door at that statement. The outlaws leaped into the car, then pushed the safe from the rear of the express car toward the open door. Using dynamite with a short fuse, the outlaws blew the door away, finding the contents safe and sound. The robbery netted them about forty thousands dollars worth of Helena National Bank notes, unsigned. A posse was quickly formed, to no avail. By the time the lawmen had reached the scene of the robbery, the bandits were safe in their hideaway.

Curses of outrage rent the air when the bandits discovered that the bills were unsigned, therefore useless. Finally, it was agreed that the outlaws would sign the banknotes themselves, most of them being signed by Ben Kilpatrick. It is said that Butch soaked the new bills in coffee to give them an aged appearance, placed them in the sun to dry and then divided the loot among his men.

Ben Kilpatrick and Laura Bullion, who had previously been the common law wife of Bill Carver prior to his death, went to St. Louis, Missouri, where they took up residence. Soon stolen currency began to circulate. The pair was arrested on November 5, 1901, and later tried at the fall term of court, and found guilty of forgery, rather than robbery, which was a strange turn of events. However, the prosecuting attorney believed he had no case against them in the matter of the train holdup, since it would have been a difficult thing to prove the prisoners had been present. Even today, Laura's and Ben's blotters exist in the files of the St. Louis Police Department showing the crime of forgery. Oddly enough, Laura also gave her name as Della Rose, alias Casey and Bullion. Ben did not bother about aliases. Ben was sentenced to fifteen years in the federal prison at Atlanta, Georgia; Laura was to serve a term of five years in the prison at Jefferson City, Tennessee.

Laura Bullion was released from prison in March 1906, and soon took to operating a boardinghouse at 87 Cental Avenue, Atlanta, Georgia, the building being opposite the prison where Kilpatrick was confined. Laura awaited anxiously the release of her lover. The Pinkertons did not. They predicted that he would be in serious trouble before too long, and their observation was correct.

While Laura was in Atlanta, Ben Kilpatrick was smuggled a note by Harvey Logan, who in turn smuggled a note out of prison to Laura which read, "The Kid is trying to locate C. (Cassidy) and get out of the country." Logan (Kid Curry) next appeared in the West carrying out another robbery to acquire funds to reach Cassidy in Argentina.

Ben Kilpatrick was released from prison on June 11, 1911, but Laura was not there to greet him. Apparently she had decided to visit South America also. Ben figured he would help the cause by robbing another train.

Down in the Devil's River country in Texas, near the Mexican border, where most of the outlaws felt safe from the law, Ben and his old buddy, Ole Beck, decided to hold up the Southern Pacific Express near Sanderson. On March 13, 1912, the two bandits boarded the train at San Angelo, anxious to take over the express car which was under the care of David A. Truesdale, a young Wells Fargo employee. Ben had learned that the safe contained a fortune in currency and other valuables.

The two outlaws broke into the express car, both armed with rifles. Ben attempted to open the safe, while Beck went to the adjoining car to rifle the mail bags. While looking over a package, Ben made the fatal mistake of taking his eye off the express messenger for a brief second. Truesdale seized a heavy mallet used for crushing ice and struck Ben on the head, smashing his skull. Ole Beck, impatient at not receiving a reply to his call to Ben, looked through the doorway. Truesdale blasted him into eternity with Ben's revolver.

In Sanderson, the brave messenger was hailed a hero. The bodies of Beck and Kilpatrick, after having been photographed, were buried in the local cemetery quickly thereafter.

It is unknown as to when Laura arrived in South America, but she was there in 1907 in the company of George Kilpatrick. Laura wanted to purchase a ranch and a new life for herself and Ben when he was released. She joined a gang which then consisted of the Sundance Kid (alias Bob Evans, alias Bud Evans), Harvey Logan (alias Andrew Duffy, alias Hood), a young man believed to have been Lew McCarty (alias William, or Willie Wilson), Harry Nation, Dick Clifford, Tom Dilly, Ansel Gibbons, George Kilpatrick, and others.

In August 1911, three bandits rode into Mercedes with plans to rob the bank. The three outlaws were later found to be two men and a woman, the latter dressed in male attire. Pinkertons later identified the three as being Butch Cassidy, Harry Longabaugh, and Etta Place, based on a report filed by their agent, Frank Dimaio. Laura Bullion was holding the horses when something went wrong inside the bank. As a result, all three bandits were shot down in the dusty streets of Villa de Mercedes. Most reports have claimed this to be Mercedes, Uruguay, but investigation in South America proved the town to be Villa de Mercedes in Argentina.

The identity of the three killed proved them to be Johnny Dey, Tom Dilly, and Laura Bul-

lion. We wonder if Ben Kilpatrick knew that his Laura had preceded him in death. Maybe; maybe not.

In any event, Elza Lay and Matt Warner were concerned about the identities of the slain robbers, and with the aid of friends, paid J. K. Bracken and Joe Walker, both of whom knew Cassidy and Longabaugh intimately, to learn the truth. They returned with the information as stated.

On December 3, 1901, Harvey Logan (Kid Curry) was arrested in Knoxville, Tennessee, with a large amount of forged notes in his possession. The following November, Curry was convicted of train robbery and sentenced to twenty years in the federal prison at Columbus, Ohio. Curry's attorneys immediately appealed his case to the sixth circuit, United States Court of Appeals. Curry knew his case was hopeless, but he bided his time.

On Saturday, June 27, 1903, Curry made his escape from the Knoxville jail by tricking guard Frank Irwin into looking out of the window overlooking the river. The Kid quickly threw a wire he had gotten from an old broom over the guard's head, slamming him back against the cell bars. Tying the wire ends to the bars, Curry left the guard in a dangerous position, the wire cutting into his throat. Kid Curry then used a makeshift line of torn pieces of cloth and a piece of wire to drag a shoebox over to the bars. The box contained two revolvers. Logan then took another guard under his guns, walked to the stables, saddled up a horse and leisurely rode down Prince Street. He decided the eastern climate did not agree with his health, so he headed back west.

Camella Hanks met his end in San Antonio, Texas, on April 16, 1902, while resisting arrest.

Butch Cassidy had gone to South America via a tramp steamer from Galveston, Texas, meeting the Sundance Kid and Etta in Buenos Aires, at the Europa Hotel. There, the outlaws and Etta filed for a government piece of land in the Province of Chubut. By the middle of 1903, they had a thriving ranch stocked with cattle, sheep, and horses.

But the Pinkerton Detective Agency had not been idle. Their crack agent, Frank P.

Dimaio, was in Brazil after a notorious jewel thief when he received a cablegram ordering him to discontinue his search and to proceed to Buenos Aires. There, another cablegram instructed him to arrest Butch Cassidy, Etta Place, and Harry Longabaugh, posing as ranchers in Chubut Province. It was quite a shock to the detective. But in checking carefully and thoroughly here and there, he learned the cablegram was authentic.

The outlaws learned through friends that the detectives were in Argentina. Disposing of their property before the law could close in on them, the three fugitives went to Chile, then into Bolivia. Just prior to leaving Argentina, the trio held up and robbed the Bank of Nacion, at Villa Mercedes, San Luis, about six hundred miles from the capital city. This occurred in March 1906.

Believing it wise to part company, Butch headed south, leaving Harry and Etta to travel into Chile, with the three to meet later at an appointed place in Santiago. Other robberies occurred which were blamed on the three Americans. One was at Bahia Blanca, Argentina, where the bank was robbed of some twenty thousand dollars; another was the holdup and robbery of the mine pay train near Eucaliptus Station.

Into Bolivia rode the bandits. There they took employment with the firm of Penny & Duncan at the Huanuhia silver mines. They tired soon of the monotony of this work and resigned. Another complication set in; Etta Place was ill. She said she had appendicitis. Harry was frantic. There were no facilities for such an emergency; he must get her back to the states for an operation. Quick inquiries told them no ship was available to the states, but one was going shortly to London. With the brazen nerve that characterized their every move, they booked passage on the steamer as Mr. and Mrs. Harry Place and James Ryan, New York City. Some claim that Butch Cassidy did not board the *North Star* that day, but remained in South America. However, it is believed, with good evidence , that both Butch and Harry accompanied Etta to Denver, Colorado, where the successful operation was performed. They then rented her a house in

Rock Springs, Wyoming, where she lived until 1909. She then made her way back to South America to join Butch and Harry.

After leaving Etta at the Denver hospital, Butch and Harry returned to South America, going into Bolivia, and spending some time in a hideout near the Inca gold mines. They took various jobs to keep them busy and from being suspected as the terrible American bandits. They worked once at the Concordia Tin Mines southeast of La Paz, where Butch became good friends with the managers of the mines, Clement Glass and Percy Seibert.

When the mines closed in 1909, Butch and Harry went to work for James and Harry Hutchinson, who were raising barley at Rio Marquez. James Hutchinson stated later that Butch told him that he and the Sundance Kid would never be taken alive. They had agreed upon a pact that, if one of them were wounded, the other was to kill him and then commit suicide.

The last robbery attributed to Butch and Harry in Bolivia occured shortly after they went to work for the Hutchinson brothers, when they robbed the mule train of its payroll for the Alpoca Silver Mines. The two robbers went to San Vicente, fifteen miles from the scene of the robbery. Their big mistake was that they carried the stolen silver coin on the back of a mule which bore the brand of the Alpoca Mines. San Vicente was a small Indian village nearly surrounded by a high wall, the interior of which was comprised of a number of native houses. At one of these, the two bandits stopped for lunch, seating themselves at a table just outside the doorway.

A local citizen, on seeing the Alpoca Mines mule, recognized it and rode to report the matter to a troop of Bolivian cavalry a mile or so down the road. The soldiers returned, racing into the interior of the wall, demanding the surrender of the Americans.

Butch and Harry ran for the nearest hut, but as they approached it, Longabaugh spun around, shot through the chest. Butch dragged Sundance into the hut, firing his sixgun at the soldiers on the wall. Blast after blast echoed from the hut as the two outlaws sent lethal slugs as fast as they could drop hammers. Every

70

Etta Place as a small child. Her background remains confusing. Where this was taken and what year aren't known.

Evidently outlaws and their friends, like most everyone, enjoyed having their pictures made. Etta Place is on the right. Where it was taken isn't known. Neither is the identity of the other young woman.

shot counted, and Butch and Harry scored heavily during the time it took the soldiers to flee to safety.

Quickly reorganizing his men, Captain Agular ordered them to stations surrounding the hut. Darkness settled, with the two outlaws still holding their fort. Both men, however, had sustained injuries; Longabaugh lay groaning, a slug in the chest, another in the groin, and a gash in his arm. Butch was luckier; he had so far just been nicked.

The sun was scarcely an hour old when the persistant captain shouted, "Surrender, senors!"

Oppressive silence followed. Nothing had been heard during the night but a single shot from the hut. The bugle sounded the charge and into the hut dashed the troopers. No one opposed them. They found both men dead.

"Madre de Dios!" cried the captain, as he pointed to a powder-burned hole between the eyes of Butch Cassidy. Apparently Harry had died, and Butch saved the last cartridge for

himself. According to legend, both bodies were buried in a small Indian cemetery a mile from town.

Of course, the deaths of Cassidy and Longabaugh come to us in a romanticized version, and also with a better trail of research. The most accepted version of their deaths is the one popularized by the 1969 movie starring Paul Newman and Robert Redford, the script taken from an account published by Arthur Chapman in *Elks Magazine,* April, 1930. According to Chapman's graphic account, Cassidy and the Sundance Kid both died in the little mountain village of San Vicente, Bolivia, in 1909. This was the first published report of the death of Butch Cassidy and the Sundance Kid. The information, according to Chapman, was obtained from Percy Seibert, an acquaintance of Cassidy who operated the Concordia Tin Mines in Bolivia.

Following the Chapman account, newspapers such as the *New York Times,* the *Washington*

Post, the *Denver Post,* and other published similar versions from Chapman's information, and the story became widely accepted as fact. Authors picked it up and published it in histories of the Wild Bunch, notably *The Outlaw Trail* by Charles Kelly in 1938, and thereafter, without any proof whatsoever, it became accepted fact.

There never was a battle at San Vincente, Bolivia, and no one was killed in a gunfight at that place in 1909 or any other time. Contemporary news accounts and official records reveal nothing of this nature ever happening there.

President Rene Berrientos of Bolivia was an astute student of the American West, having gone to school in the states before rising in the politics of his country. While giving a speech on the subject, he was asked by an American observer to prove the statement that Butch and the Kid had been killed in San Vicente, and President Berrientos set out in 1960 to do just that. Instead, he proved the opposite.

Dr. Tornapolski, a noted physician, was flown to San Vicente, accompanied by Berrientos and others, and an exhumation of the only two foreign bodies was made in the local cemetery. It was proved that neither had died of bullet wounds and that they had been buried as much as fourteen years apart.

Not satisfied, Berrientos even checked the official records and interviewed living witnesses, but no record appeared of such a gunfight having occurred there. Indeed, there was not even a Bolivian cavalry outpost within three hundred miles of San Vicente, and the only police officer in the tiny village had one rifle and no ammunition.

How then, had the story started in the first place? Percy Seibert, the good and loyal friend of Butch Cassidy, had seen an opportunity to help his friends escape the country and had concocted the story for the benefit of the Pinkertons and others who came to his tin mines seeking the whereabouts of the "Norte Americanos bandios."

When Butch Cassidy was supposed to have been killed at San Vicente, he and the Kid were in the United States . . . in Utah . . .

and Cassidy was seeking a new life and a new identity. His recent "death" gave him this opportunity.

In 1929, a man by the name of William T. Phillips began to cast about, seeking some of the old caches left by Cassidy, in the vain hope of salvaging his business in Spokane, Washington, during the depression. In his zeal, and having ridden with Cassidy in earlier years, some people mistook him for Cassidy.

Cassidy was living nearby at the time and the curiosity seekers were endangering his identity. He conferred with Arthur Chapman, who was a personal friend, and with his friend Percy Seibert, then residing in Santiago, Chile, and the revived story of the demise of Butch and Sundance appeared in the *Elks Magazine,* as stated. It was highly publicized throughout the country, and copies were sent to hundreds of people throughout the United States by Percy Seibert. This, of course, belayed any suspicion to the contrary, assuring Butch his safety. Eyewitness-notarized-statements exist as to the exhumation of the bodies at San Vicente, Bolivia.

True, there were two American outlaws killed in Mercedes, Argentina, in the summer of 1911, together with a woman, whom some have erroneously believed to have been Etta Place. The men who were killed were former outlaws from the United States, loose-knit members of the Wild Bunch named Tom Dilly and Johnny Dey. The woman was Laura Bullion. Perhaps this incident gave Percy Seibert the basis for his false story.

The Sundance Kid died in Salt Lake City, Utah, in 1955, under the alias of Hiram Beebe. He had killed a marshal in Utah and was serving time in prison when he died. He was buried in a pauper's grave in the Salt Lake City Cemetery.

From his own letters to his sister, Lula Parker Betenson, and to Mrs. Matt Warner, we learn that Butch kept busy during years still left to him. His last letter to Mrs. Warner was dated June 24, 1940, and was postmarked Goldfield, Nevada. Butch was involved with Pancho Villa during the revolution in Mexico, as was Etta Place. In 1937 he worked with his daughter, Thelma Topping Beene, and his son-in-law

This is believed to be Butch Cassidy's grave, near Johnny, Nevada. There are several versions as to how Cassidy died, none of which is proved out.

in a mine in Nevada, using an alias while employed as a guard at the mine. Butch was killed in 1941 when a cable broke at the mine, toppling an eight foot iron wheel on him. He was buried next to Bob Parker, a close relative, whose full name probably was Robert Parker McMullin. As he had requested, Butch was buried at Johnny, Nevada, head-to-foot, facing north instead of east. As his daughter said, Butch always considered that the north star had been his guide in life, and he wanted to face it on the morning of the Resurrection.

Kerry Ross Boren, a noted Utah historian and friend of the late Lula Parker Betenson, provided the author a photo of Butch taken in Mexico, as well as some of this important new material.

Harold Thayn Longabaugh, who said he was Harry's son, stated that Sundance was not killed in Bolivia. He stated he met his father at the Chicago Hotel in Spokane, Washington, in 1940. Also that he had been born several weeks before Cassidy, Longabaugh, and Etta Place went to South America. He also stated that his mother was Anna Marie Thayn, daughter of Johnson Thayn, a polygamist of

Castle Dale, Utah. He stated mistakingly that Etta Place was really named Thayn, but this occurred because Etta was living at the Johnson Thayn home for a time, and while there, used the name of Ethel Thayn.

Etta's real name was Etta Place, she taking the family name after being born out of wedlock to Emily Jane Place and George Capel, alias Ingerfield, the illegitimate son of Arthur Algernon Capel, sixth earl of Essex. This event caused the family much embarrassment, so George Capel was sent to live with his step-uncle, Richard Boyle, ninth earl of Cork. There he was given management over certain estates by his uncle. However, his cruel reputation forced him to flee Ireland under threat of assassination.

George Capel went west and lived with his friend, Moreton Frewen, in Kansas, but a short time later, we find him at the Frewen ranch on Powder River in Wyoming. During his frequent forays in New York, George Capel became enamored with a young aspiring actress named Emily Jane Place. As a result she became pregnant with his child and Capel speedily left for the West. Etta's mother was a near relative to the mother of Harry Alonzo Longabaugh, Annie G. Place Longabaugh (Josiah), and in fact, was Harry's cousin, not his lover, as most claim.

Whatever happened to Etta Place is a moot question. All practical traces of her are lost after 1929 when she was then living at 619 Ohio Street, Denver, Colorado, according to the Ballinger and Richard's Directory, of that city. In the late 1950s, Queen Anne Bassett Willis was residing at Leeds, Utah, in the house of one of Cassidy's cousins — the McMullins — when she claims Etta Place visited her. Rumors persisted that in the 1960s, she was living with a niece and nephew, well into her nineties.

Perhaps it was true, for as late as 1971, as Etta's daughter Bettie lay dying of cancer in a hospital in the Northwest, she informed her husband, "Mother may still be living. She remarried and may have had other children."

The final curtain on the life of Etta Place probably drew to a close somewhere in or near Denver, Colorado.

Chapter Eight

Burton Mossman, Savior of Arizona

WHEN THE Territorial Legislature of Arizona passed Act 74 with its various sections on March 21, 1901, it brought into being one of the bravest and hardest fighting group of men ever to ride the border. This group was known as the Arizona Rangers; it was the finest body of men ever recruited for service on the frontier. They were picked men enlisted from the hundreds of fearless cowboys of the territory, who were skilled in riding, trailing, and shooting. The personnel of the ranger force was kept secret from the general public, and the presence of a body of rangers in a community seldom was known until their work was completed.

The Arizona Rangers consisted of one captain, one sergeant, and not more than twelve privates, each enlisted to the following salary: captain received $120 per month; sergeant was paid $75 a month; and the pay of the privates was $55 per month. Later, the legislative assembly passed a bill calling for the rangers to consist of one captain, one lieutenant, four sergeants, and not more than twenty privates. The pay was raised also: captain, $175 a month; lieutenant, $130 a month; sergeants, $110 a month; and privates, $100 a month.

The first captain of the famous Arizona Rangers was Burton C. Mossman, a man in his early thirties, who feared nothing, had often stared death in the face, and came out fighting. Yet, Burton had not really wanted the ranger's commission, but felt that he owed Arizona something.

Mossman was a young man of twenty-one when he was made foreman of the mighty Bar N Cross Ranch. Burton was working on the ranch as a bog rider, whose duty it was to rescue the cattle which strayed into the treacherous quicksand. The boy's honesty and perserverance made a great impression on his employer. Mossman and Warren Carpenter, younger brother of the owner of the Bar N, and who, himself, was owner of the Bar A Ranch, became great friends. Young Mossman's heart was filled with sorrow that evening in 1888, for his friend, Warren, had been killed by lightning the past August.

"Warren never regretted the day he hired you on the Bar A; I'm sure that you'll do just as fine a job for me on the Bar N," Andy Carpenter told his young foreman.

Burton Mossman managed to gulp out his thanks to his new boss, striving valiantly to hide back a few tears which managed to show through his sorrow over the loss of Warren Carpenter. Mossman was also greatly concerned about the lack of water for the thousands of cattle that roamed the great ranches of the area.

After leaving the Carpenter ranch, Mossman allowed his mount to drift at will until he neared Canada Alamosa, then deciding to visit the little village of Monticello, where he thought to quench his thirst with a cold beer. The young man refused to touch anything stronger than beer.

Yes, this was Burton C. Mossman, resolute

and determined to make a niche in life for himself, selecting a locality where only the strong could survive. Mossman was the son of Maj. Mossman of the Union Army, born on April 30, 1867, on an Illinois farm near Aurora. When he was still a lad, the Mossmans moved to Lake City, Minnesota. From that point, young Burt and his father drove covered wagons to his father's two land claims near Marshall, near the Dakota border.

At the age of sixteen, Burton decided that farming was not his work, so he hired out to a surveying crew in the Sacramento Mountains, near the Tularosa Basin. Later, he went to work for the owner of the Little Hat Ranch, but decided to leave there after a short time, for he had become involved in some personal grudges with one of the cowboys. He feared tempers might flare to a point where someone would get killed, and the young man did not believe a job was worth that price.

Soon after leaving the Little Hat Ranch, Burton met Warren Carpenter, who hired him to work on the Bar A Bar, one of the largest ranches in the Territory of New Mexico.

As Mossman rode up the village of Monticello, he viewed the shabby buildings and their awesome shapes cast across the blistering sands, and it added more misery to his depressed state. He dismounted in front of the local saloon, tired and hot, tied his mount to the hitch-rack, and started to enter the building. As he did so, he heard angry voices in the bar. As Burt walked through the dangling batwing doors, he saw a Mexican named Lopez taunting a harmless sheepherder named Juan Reyes.

Should he get involved? But the character of Mossman was such that he was speaking before he probably realized it.

"What's the matter with Lopez? You should know better than to pick on such a harmless critter."

"You want some, too?" rasped the Mexican bully, as he swung at Mossman. Burt sidestepped and struck the man a stunning blow in the face. The Mexican seemed to lose all sense of reason as he reached for his knife and lunged at the youthful Burt.

A hard blow on the chin landed Lopez on the floor, sawdust and antiquated furniture going in all directions. Burt leaped on top of the man, grabbing his knife hand. Another blow to Lopez's chin limbered him up long

Arizona Historical Society Library
The first captain of the famed Arizona Rangers was Burton C. Mossman, who was in his thirties when he took on the job.

enough to enable Burt to clamp a strong hold on the man's throat.

"Let him up, Burt, you'll kill him sure," warned one of his friends.

But Burt hung on like a bulldog. Then finally persuaded to loosen his hold on the man's neck, the Mexican's tongue was hanging out of his mouth and his face was already turning purple.

Burt's Mexican friend warned him about Lopez, telling him that the bully would want revenge and for Burt to be on the alert all the time.

"Don't worry about me, amigo; it was a fair fight, and I enjoyed it," Mossman told his friend. "It was something different for a change."

Busy as he was, Mossman soon forgot about the Lopez incident until one evening when he was seated at his desk and had risen from his chair to stretch his weary back. At that very instant, a heavy calibre slug tore through the window and followed a path where, but a few moments before, the boy's head had been. Some sixth sense had warned Mossman to move at just the right time.

Burt knew that Lopez was responsible for the ambush, but, of course, he had no way to prove it. Several days later, Lopez was killed at Bourgett's vineyard near the Anchor X Ranch by Bill Hardin, cousin of the famed gunman, John Wesley Hardin. The two had been hitting the wine bottle for hours when Lopez, in his usual ugly mood, started an argument and drew his knife, slashing at Hardin. Bill simply shot him between the eyes, and that was the end of that. Even though Hardin was drunk, he realized that one of Lopez's friends would be gunning for him, so he beat a hasty retreat toward the Anchor X. He never made it. He was ambushed and killed by a Mexican named Juan Boca.

The news did not disturb Mossman very much. He was worried about the lack of rain. Not a drop had fallen in months; the water holes dried up, and the cattle became thin and listless. Burt realized it was time to take the cattle to Dodge City, and also have a talk with the Lankford brothers, co-owners of the ranch he managed. This would mean a stopover at Pueblo, Colorado, on his return trip from Dodge.

The cattle driven safely to Dodge City, Mossman made his way to Pueblo, where he consulted with the Lankfords, who instructed him to locate a possible buyer for the Bar A Ranch, which they also owned. Unable to find a buyer due to the drought, Mossman himself managed to raise three thousand five hundred dollars and bought the ranch. But still the rains failed to come; things got worse for Burt, and he was forced to board up his buildings and head for San Marcial. Much to his dislike, Burt took employment there as a bookkeeper.

But office work was not for Burt. He could not stand the monotony and the inactivity, so in a short while, he took a train for Chicago, where he visited the Chicago Exposition. Burt had left a forwarding address with the postmaster in New Mexico for his mail to be sent to a friend's home in Chicago, should any arrive. At the home of his friend, Mossman found a letter awaiting him from Frank Bloom, a cattleman from Trinidad, Colorado. The letter suggested the matter of a business transaction between the two men, so it was not long before Burt was in Mr. Bloom's office.

"You did a fine job for the Lankford brothers in New Mexico, I understand. The Thatcher boys and I are interested in about fifteen thousand head of cattle scattered in the rough country north of Phoenix. The owners are deeply in debt to our banks. Would you be willing to work for us in getting this matter straightened out?"

Burton was pleasantly surprised and quickly replied, "I'll certainly give the try my best efforts."

Late in 1893, Mossman arrived in the Bloody Basin country and made a close inspection of the area. He was given all the necessary cooperation by the three men indebted to Bloom and his associates. These rugged men were Granville Graybeal, D. L. Murphy, and Walter Hudson. They all agreed with Burt that the problem was to steer a large number of cattle through the great cholla cactus, the mesquite, and other heavy underbrush. Nearly every accessible path ended at the base of a thousand foot high cliff.

"We've got to conquer the Mogollon Rim if we are to ever move these cattle out," Burt told his workers. "We may have to do it in single file." His words proved to be prophetic.

Days went by as Burt and his foreman, Hayden Justice, rode the territory, seeking a feasible way to leave the basin. Also, the round-up continued, and soon a sufficient number of cattle would be on hand to start the drive to Flagstaff. How to get them out of the basin was the question.

"We might try the old military road that General Crook built some years back," suggested Hayden.

The men looked at him as if he were out of his mind. They all agreed that the road would probably be washed out by now, since it had not been used since General Crook was at Camp Verde. Yet they all also agreed it was the best suggestion that had been offered to date.

It was a difficult job to move several thousand cattle to the base of the old army road. Burt scratched his head as he peered up at the old trail. The road looked as though it could hardly hold a man on horseback, much less cattle. Little by little, the cattle were driven over the treacherous road in small groups. By nightfall, the entire herd had been brought out of the basin. Burt and his men had performed a feat unparalleled in the annals of cattle history.

It was a full month before cattle cars arrived at Clark's Valley from Flagstaff to remove the cattle to the shipping pens. Mossman had done a good job, but even for a man like him, the Basin country had been too rough, so he resigned.

Mossman was not idle long. The story of his work in removing the cattle from the basin had reached the ears of the president of the Aztec Land and Cattle Company, owners of the Hash Knife spread in Arizona Territory, and in December of 1897 Burt was offered the job of managing the huge outfit.

Only thirty years of age, Burt thought he might have bitten off more than he could chew. The Hash Knife owned over fifty thousand head of cattle and covered over a million acres of land, running from eighty miles west of Holbrook and forty miles to the south of the railroad. The mighty outfit also controlled another million acres of railroad property.

On January 20, 1898 Mossman alighted from the train car at Holbrook, Arizona. The Hash Knife headquarters were at Joseph City, a short distance from town, but Mossman wanted to speak to the newly-elected sheriff in town, since he had heard that the Hash Knife people were using gunmen and killers in their outfit.

Frank Wattron was the new sheriff. He had defeated the Hash Knife outfit candidate John Jones, its general manager, in a very close and bitter race, winning the election by seven votes. Wattron had been a Justice of the Peace and was always called "judge." After the election, Jones left the territory, Mossman being the man to replace him.

Navajo County was a mecca for rustlers. For over fifteen years, wholesale rustling was practiced and not one conviction is on record for that period. Not only that, but this caused the Hash Knife stockholders to lose well over one hundred thousand dollars.

The cowboy who met Mossman at the train was congenial and very talkative.

"We had a report that some renegade Mormons were butchering some Hash Knife stock over at Winslow."

"What's your name?"

"Charley Fought," the young man told Mossman.

"Well, we ought to check that first. I was going to have a long talk with the sheriff, but I'll pass that up for now."

The two cold riders had covered thirty miles by dusk and were nearing Snowflake, when they came upon three men seated close to a roaring fire. The two men could see a wagon-load of stolen beef nearby. They noted also that each man held a rifle in his hands, ready for instant action.

Mossman whispered to his companion, "Watch the men and act accordingly."

"Damned cold evening, mind if we use your fire?" remarked Burt, as he strolled into camp with his friend.

The three rustlers made no reply. Apparently they were fooled by the large dude overcoat Mossman was wearing, also thinking little of the unimpressive appearance of his young companion.

Suddenly, Mossman drew his revolver from his overcoat pocket and jabbed it into the back of the man nearest him.

"Drop your guns or this man dies."

The rifles clattered to the ground.

"Keep them covered, Charley, and if any of them make a move, shoot him," instructed Mossman.

Near the wagon, Mossman· found several cattle hides bearing the Hash Knife brand. The three rustlers were herded into Holbrook, along with the beef and hides as evidence. Later, the leader of the rustlers was found guilty of grand larceny and sentenced to five years in the territorial prison, the maximum penalty at that time for rustling.

With his prisoners safely lodged in the town jail, Mossman looked up Sheriff Wattron, and the two men had a long talk.

"Mossman, just how far will you go with me in this matter?"

"As far as you will and farther if need be."

"That's good enough for me. Here's your deputy sheriff commission and your badge. I'll give you my best man, Joe Bargeman, to assist you."

Although the men he had arrested were renegade Mormons, Burt wanted to speak with the bishop of the Latter-day Saints Church to get his true feelings in the matter of the rustlers. The first thing he did was to visit Snowflake and arrange a meeting with the bishop.

"Bishop, how do you feel about this cattle stealing business?"

"I am against it, and so is my church."

"Fine, then I'm going to ask for an entire Mormon jury to decide the fate of the men I arrested."

To say that the bishop was surprised would be putting it mildly. He was stunned. He well knew that a mixed jury would free the rustlers, but the bishop stood by his word and the cattle thieves were convicted by a Mormon jury.

Mossman analyzed the situation well when he decided that he had a three-pronged prob-

lem relative to the rustlers. He felt that the wholesale rustling was being committed by renegade Mormons, Mexicans, and Hash Knife employees themselves, or ex-employees. Burt's resolute and determined decision to rid the range of rustlers had the desired effect upon many of the stealing cowboys. Some of them left the area, and some were arrested and sent to prison. Still the rustling continued, with Mossman realizing finally that the major part of the stealing had been done by Mexicans.

One morning he talked to Deputy Bargeman about it, and asked if he wanted to trap some Mexican rustlers in Water Canyon.

"That's the territory of that damned outlaw Baca and his men. I've had a run-in with him before; he's bad medicine, but I'll tag along," replied Bargeman.

Late in the afternoon, the two officers rode up in front of several cabins in the bottom of the canyon. Before one of the cabins loitered six Mexicans. Burt and his companion dismounted, rifles ready in their hands.

"We're from the sheriff's office and we want to search these cabins for stolen beef," Mossman told the one man who appeared to be the leader of the group.

"No search anything if you no have warrant."

Burt was taken back. Evidently someone had put these outlaws wise to the law. But Mossman was equal to the situation. He took an official looking paper from his pocket and handed it to the outlaw, who proved to be Baca.

The outlaw stared at the paper, saying nothing. Just as Mossman had guessed, the man could not read.

"The first cabin is empty, Burt, and the second one is paddlocked."

"I'll guard this fellow; get an axe and break down the door."

Mossman expected no trouble from the other men, who had drifted into the shadows of the trees. When the door of the second cabin had been smashed open, they found quarters of beef hanging from the ceiling inside.

"Just as I thought," said Mossman, as he peered into the cabin. At the same time, Baca dashed across the clearing toward a scrub-covered mesa.

"Stop!" cried Mossman. "Or I'll kill you!"

Baca and Mossman scrambled up the slope to a rim on the edge of the mesa. There, Mossman saw a young man racing from the cover of the trees, a rifle in his hand. His intentions were plain; he was hoping to arm Baca. Still Mossman did not shoot. He raced up to Baca and struck him over the head with a gun barrel. One of Baca's men fired but missed.

"Dammit, Baca, tell your men to stop shooting or you're a dead man."

Just then, Bargeman came up and gave chase to the men in the trees. Mossman forced his prisoner back to the cabins and placed him in one in which there were no windows, carefully blocking the door.

The next morning, with the prisoner in tow with a rope around his neck, Mossman and Bargeman forced Baca to the cabin where his men were. Burt placed a revolver to Baca's head and told him he would kill him if he did not tell his men to surrender.

The cabin door opened slowly and four disgruntled Mexicans filed out, hands high in the air. The five prisoners were taken to Holbrook, where they were placed in the jail. Yet Mossman was puzzled. The Mexicans had been able to destroy all evidence of cattle rustling, yet they seemed worried about something else.

"You know, sheriff, I'll bet they were stealing horses also," Burt remarked.

"I believe you are right."

It was discovered that one of the prisoners had tried to smuggle a note from the jail. It read "Muevele los caballos" — move the horses.

Mossman, Bargeman and several more officers combed the Water Canyon country, searching for hidden horses. Finally, they located sixteen fine farm animals which had been stolen from the Salt River Valley farmers.

The five prisoners and three others appeared that fall in the court of Judge Sloan. They were tried by an honest jury, for a change; all were found guilty and sentenced from two to five years in the hell-hole prison at Yuma.

Mossman saw to it personally that the prisoners were safely delivered to that miserable prison squatted on the banks of the Colorado River. Mossman stopped off at Phoenix to see some old friends on his return trip. He spoke also with Governor Murphy.

"Burt," said the governor, "you are doing a grand job, but you still have organized crime to buck. I mean Bill Young and his gang around Holbrook. You should organize a larger police enforcement group."

"Wattron and Mossman is all the organization we need right now," Burt assured the governor.

Late in 1898, Frank Wattron and Burt Mossman went on a little hunting trip. They felt good about how things were going. The Hash Knife people had praised their work, and much of the rustling had stopped.

One morning the two hunters awoke at their camp on Chevron Creek to find a foot of snow on the ground.

"Good Lord, Frank, this will kill the cattle. Let's get back to Holbrook," cried Mossman.

Wattron was more hopeful. "Maybe it's just a December passing storm," he said.

But it was not. For weeks the snow piled up under a dark sky which refused to allow the sun to shine through. When the snow had reached its tenth week, Mossman wrote his superiors that the cattle loss would be great, at least ten thousand head.

The company officials assured Mossman there was nothing he could have done to prevent this tragedy. Later, it was learned that the receipts from the cattle sales under Burt's supervision had still exceeded what the owners of the Hash Knife had expected.

When the blizzard and the cattle drives were over, Mossman and Bargeman returned to hunting rustlers. One day, Mossman received a message from the Bishop of Snowflake that some men had driven a small herd through town, and he suspected that the animals had been stolen.

After an all night ride, the two officers arrived at the bishop's home. However, in fear of retaliation toward the bishop, they were shown the rustlers' trail just at the break of day, so they could not be seen.

The trail led east along a rough wagon road,

then up a canyon which separated a mesa on the left from higher mountains on the right. To avoid being seen, the deputies left the trail and went up over the bench. They rode silently and cautiously, well-knowing that a rustler camp could not be far distant. A half mile farther up the canyon, they came upon the camp.

The two trailers found concealment on the lip of the rimrock and watched the camp through their glasses. They recognized several notorious cattle thieves among the men at the camp, and Bargeman was ready for an instant attack. But the cool head of Mossman prevailed and the men waited.

"Dammit, Burt, my canteen is about empty and I don't aim to die of thirst on account of those rustlers."

"Quit kicking, Joe. We'll creep down to that cool spring over there after it gets dark and fill up our canteens."

It was well past midnight when the two officers crept down to the spring and replenished their water supply. The next day, they again took up their vigil, creeping nearer to the corral where the outlaws were branding the stolen stock.

"There are five of them," whispered Joe.

"Right, but I'm interested in that young fellow who takes the same trail up the canyon all the time."

Ignoring the men at the camp, Mossman and Bargeman slipped across the main canyon and followed the trail taken by the youth. Suddenly, they saw a small corral filled with calves. It was now apparent that this young man had been given the duty of taking care of these animals.

The boy was seated on the edge of the spring and nearly fell into the water when Burt and Joe walked up to him, so great was his surprise on seeing them.

"We're hunters, son, and want some grub; no need to get alarmed," Burt said.

"You can't fool me, you're officers," replied the boy.

"All right, then, we are going to your camp, and if you make any warning sound, you'll be killed."

It was near dusk when they neared the camp, and they saw only two of the rustlers seated by the fire.

"Hands up!" cried Burt.

The startled rustlers leaped to their feet, hands high in the air. Joe disarmed and tied them hand and foot. He then dragged them into the brush to conceal them. It was now a waiting game until the remaining two thieves returned to their camp.

It was well after dark when the other two rustlers arrived and walked right into the trap. The next morning all five rustlers were placed in the wagon found at the camp. They were driven into Holbrook, where they were later convicted and received sentences ranging from two to three years. Mossman spoke to the judge in behalf of the young man, and as a result, the youth was placed on probation. Mossman said that the Yuma prison was no place for the young boy.

Even though by now most of the big-scale rustling had stopped, Mossman had never been able to convict the last of the big operators, Bill Young.

"I've had enough of this Hash Knife outfit and that damned Mossman," Young remarked. "I'm leaving Arizona and moving to Colorado."

Burt told Young later that his idea was a good one; the sooner he left, the better. Also, he told Young that he had been a hard adversary.

True to his word, Young did leave Arizona, moving to Rifle, Colorado. However, it was not long before he was again in trouble. He had killed a man in an argument and had been sentenced to twenty years in the Colorado State Prison.

In the spring of 1900, Mossman received orders to close out the Hash Knife holdings, and he did just that, showing a nice profit to boot. He then went to Phoenix and stayed at the Palace Hotel. There, he met Col. Bill Greene, rich many times over from the profits of his copper mines in Sonora. Colonel Greene tried to persuade Mossman to join forces with him in handling his cattle matters, but Burt refused, stating that he was fed up with fighting such territory as Pleasant Valley, the Bloody Basin, and other such places.

In Phoenix, Burt also met Ed Tovrea, who was in the butcher business, and explained to Mossman and Greene that he was anxious to expand his shops. He got Mossman finally to agree to take over a partnership in the shop he was going to open in Bisbee. But the business was not to Burt's liking; he missed riding pell-mell across the plains or tracking rustlers in the mountains.

Colonel Greene cornered Mossman again and offered him the manager's job at the Colonel Hooker Ranch north of Wilcox. The colonel insisted that his count of 12,500 head of cattle be accepted when Greene bought the ranch, but Mossman wanted to see for himself. Burt rode the Hooker range for several days, finally realizing that the colonel did not have nearly such an amount of cattle. As a result, the deal fell through and Burt returned to the butcher business in Bisbee.

Things did not remain peaceful for long, however. Soon stories of holdups, train robberies, and other crimes became the talk of the day. Just as the reputation of Billy the Kid had kept people from coming into New Mexico in the late 1870s, now the Territory of Arizona was threatened with the same kind of situation.

Burton Mossman had ruled with an iron hand on the counties of Apache and Navajo, but over in Cochise County, on the border of Mexico, murders and train robberies ran rampant. Augustin Chacon, a noted Mexican bandit, had killed over thirty Americans, but conditions in that area were in such a sad state of affairs that the authorities never were able to cope with the wily robber.

Governor Murphy called Mossman into his office and asked him to form some sort of peace officers unit to fight crime in Arizona.

"I want no part of this, governor. I'm just beginning to make good money for the first time in my life; besides, you have a dozen good men who can fill the bill."

"All right, Mossman, but at least you can help draft the bill."

Attorney Frank Cox of the Southern Pacific and Mossman worked at the Hotel Adams for weary hours until a passable bill was ham-mered out between them, which they presented to Governor Murphy.

The governor rushed it to the Territorial Secretary for presentation to the legislative assembly, and on March 21, 1901 a law was passed which brought into existence the Arizona Rangers.

Burton Mossman leaned back in his chair, a smile of satisfaction on his face; he was a satisfied man in knowing that he had done his part in the law enforcement field and having helped to draft the bill creating the rangers. Now he could concentrate on his butcher business, make a good living, and take it easy for a spell. But hardly had the bill been passed when influential friends began banging down his front door trying to entice him to accept the first captaincy of the newly-created band of peace officers.

Burt threw up his hands in resignation.

"I suppose you people will never let me rest in peace until I do," he sighed.

"That's exactly right," said Colonel Greene, while the others in the governor's office nodded in agreement.

"I want no political power to interfere with my work. I want to pick my own men, write my own ticket, take orders from nobody, and name my successor. Besides that, I'll take the job for only a year, but I doubt that I'll live that long."

Governor Murphy agreed to Burt's terms.

Captain Mossman knew that he must have the best men available, men picked with care and skill, noted for their bravery and fidelity. For his sergeant, Burt picked Dayton Graham, a Bisbee peace officer; the second man was Burt Grover, who acted at times in the capacity of sergeant. After the roster had been filled, Burton addressed his men: "First, I'd like to say that whatever you do, I'll stick by you to the end. Second, our first problem is to break up the gangs moving from Sonora into our country and stealing everything they can lay their hands on."

The rangers first assignment came when the wires hummed with the news of the holdup of the post office at Tucumcari, in eastern New Mexico, where a young boy was killed in the raid. Captain Mossman and four rangers were rushed by special train to Clifton.

Led by Bill Daniels, the hotly pursued bandits crossed the New Mexico border into Arizona. For some unknown reason, Daniels left the band, allowing five of the outlaws to ride toward the spot where Mossman and his men waited. Mossman was informed by one of the local ranchers that the outlaw camp had been sighted, and at dawn Mossman and his four rangers closed in and demanded the surrender of the bandits. Two of the men were arrested, but three escaped. J. Smith, one of the outlaws who had escaped, was later captured, while the other two outlaws were killed from ambush.

The desperate men of Arizona began to wonder about this silent and mysterious little band of avenging rangers, who dispensed justice with a swift hand. They could learn little of the group except that it was headed by that rough-and-ready man named Burton Mossman.

October brought bad news for Mossman. He was at Solomonville when he received a wire from St. Johns, signed by Henry Huning, stating that a ranger named Bill Maxwell had been killed by the Bill Smith gang, and that ranger Carlos Tefio had been critically wounded. With one ranger, Mossman hurried to Clifton, then to the forks of the Black River, where the fight had occurred. There, Captain Mossman talked to Henry Barrett, who had been a member of the ranger posse, and got the straight story from him.

The Smith gang had held up a Union Pacific train in Utah, then had stolen some horses and headed south. Barrett contacted the three rangers when he learned that the gang was holed up in a cabin on Black River. It was nearly dark when the leader of the posse called out for the gang to surrender. Bill Smith reached the safety of the cabin, but his brother raised his hands in pretense of surrender, dropping his rifle in the snow as he did so.

Ranger Carlos Tefio motioned for the outlaw to walk toward him. The robber walked forward, slowly dragging the rifle with his foot, using the shoulder strap to do so. When he came to a shallow draw, he pretended to fall.

As he did so, he grabbed his rifle and shot Tefio in the stomach. The third ranger had gone for help and Maxwell demanded that Smith surrender. Smith was an excellent shot and his answer was a bullet through the ranger's hat. Not heeding this display of marksmanship, Maxwell again peered from his hiding place; again Smith fired, the bullet striking the ranger in the eye.

Captain Mossman knew the trail was cold and too tough for him to tackle. He sent a runner to the San Carlos Indian Agency requesting the loan of two Apache scouts. Two Apache Indian policemen named Old Josh and Kid arrived the next day. The scouts did an excellent job at tracking, but the blizzards that came wiped out all traces of the outlaws' trail.

The wily Smith had crossed into Mexico at Douglas, but on learning that no one suspected his presence in the area, he returned to Douglas to enjoy some of his ill-gotten gains. At the same time, Ranger Dayton Graham was in Douglas, checking the border for signs of Smith and the outlaw Chacon.

One evening while Graham was talking with the night marshal, Tom Vaughn, a merchant came up and told Vaughn that a suspicious-looking man was seated on the steps of his store and that he wanted him removed.

The two officers walked up to the man and asked him his name. His reply was a swiftly drawn revolver and several fast-snapped shots. One bullet struck Vaughn in the neck, the other bore through the ranger's lung. Even as the stranger fled, he fired another shot, the bullet striking Graham in the arm.

Mossman was informed at Bisbee that Graham was dying. Burt hurriedly gathered the man's family in a buggy and raced them the thirty miles to Douglas. But Ranger Graham did not die. For two months he was bedridden, always plagued by the face of the coarse-haired man who had shot him.

"I'll get that sonofabitch some day, captain," he later told Mossman. From that moment on, he planned to live up to that threat.

The search for the man who had shot him became an obsession with Ranger Graham.

After he had regained his health, he rode from town to town, visited bar after bar, gambling den after gambling den, always on the alert for the stranger who had shot him in Douglas. Mossman seemed to think the matter had preyed long enough upon Graham's mind, and he was intending to transfer him to another area. But the move was not necessary. One night Graham saw his quarry seated at a monte table. The man went for his gun, but too late. The ranger's gun spewed flame and death. One slug tore through the man's head and two others hit him in the stomach.

"That will make sure you'll not kill any more officers, you sonofabitch," Graham cried.

Mossman arrived from Bisbee the next morning, and to the great satsifaction of everyone concerned, the dead man was positively identified as the outlaw, Bill Smith.

The White Mountain country was now cleared of some of its worst outlaws, giving the rangers an opportunity to work other parts of the territory. Word was received from Globe, Arizona, that cattle thieves posing at respectable citizens were selling stolen cattle to buyers in the Salt River Valley. Ranger Robinson and three assistants were sent to arrest the rustlers.

Arriving in Globe, Robinson and his men watched the area around the valley. Names of six suspects had been given to the ranger, and one day he and his men saw these six enter their ranch house. Taken completely by surprise when Robinson and his men rushed into the building, the six men surrendered without a struggle. They expressed outrage at the accusation of being cattle rustlers.

The citizens of Globe also thought their respected friends were being railroaded, and all rushed forward to place a deposit of a two thousand dollars bond set for each of the arrested men. One can imagine their surprise when the trial came up; all of the six "highly-respected members of the community" had fled across the border into Mexico. Those persons who had guaranteed the appearance of the six men at the trial clamored for the return of their bond money. Many influential people in the vicinity petitioned the governor to return the money, but he refused to do so unless Captain Mossman recommended this course of action.

"Governor, this money should not be returned," Mossman advised. "This will teach those people to think twice before putting up bail for their fine citizens in the future."

The governor was true to his word and did not return the money.

Cochise and Santa Cruz counties were next to be visited by the Arizona Rangers. Conditions in these sections were so bad that desperate measures had to be taken. Many of the county sheriffs were unfriendly toward the rangers, thinking that their presence was a reflection of their own ability to handle matters properly.

High on the arrest list were Burt Alvord and Augustin Chacon. Alvord had been raised around Tombstone, where he served for a time as an officer under the shotgun-carrying Sheriff John Slaughter. Alvord later became marshal of Willcox, where he saw a chance to grow rich quick. With outlaws Bob Downing and Billy Stiles, he robbed the express car at Cochise Junction of eighty thousand dollars in gold. The gold was hidden by Alvord, and all three planned their alibis. But Downing got drunk and told the story of the holdup.

The three outlaws were arrested and held in the jail at Tombstone. A friend smuggled a gun to Stiles. He shot jailer Bravin in the leg, secured the jail door keys, and released Downing and Alvord. In the cell next to Alvord, the Mexican killer, Chacon, was being held. Chacon pleaded with Alvord to release him, too. In reply, Alvord tossed the keys to Chacon and left him do the rest.

Alvord tried many times to dig up the hidden gold, but the officers of the county were so vigilant in their pursuit of him that he was frustrated at every effort to do so.

One day Chacon rode into Morenci in Clifton County and robbed a store, killing the owner for no apparent reason. Billy Birchfield, sheriff of Graham County, soon was in hot pursuit of Chacon, trapping him in a box canyon.

Pablo Salcido, one of the possemen, asked the sheriff if he could speak with Chacon, for they had been friends for a long time. Permission was granted, but when Salcido walked out into the open, calling to Chacon, the Mexican shot him dead. A fierce fight ensued in which Chacon was wounded twice and captured.

He was taken to Solomonville, where he was tried and sentenced to be hanged for the murder of the storekeeper named Becker. However, Chacon's wily girl friend smuggled saw blades into the cell by placing them in the thick cover of a large prayerbook. Just two days before Chacon was to be hanged, they found his cell empty.

When Mossman came to Tombstone, the people believed he was on the trail of Alvord, but he was laying desperate plans to catch Chacon. He set up a series of secret police at various posts, and also made an agreement with Col. Emilio Kosterlitzky of the Sonora Rurales in Mexico. But the cunning Chacon made sure he committed no crimes in Mexico, so Kosterlitzky refused to turn over Mexicans for United States prosecution; refugee Americans, yes.

Mossman believed he could capture Chacon with the assistance of Burt Alvord. So he contacted Alvord's half-brother in Mexico, showing him a letter written by federal district judge Barnes, which stated that Alvord would be pardoned for crimes committed in Arizona if he would consent to assist in the capture of Chacon. His secret meeting with Alvord's relative at Minas Prietas completed, Mossman rode the trail pointed out by the outlaw's half-brother.

Burt was wondering how he would approach Alvord with the proposition to betray Chacon when he suddenly turned a curve in the trail and found himself directly in front of a large stone building. He also saw a number of vicious-looking rifle barrels protruding from loopholes in the sides of the walls.

"Burt Alvord!" called Mossman.

"Who the hell are you?" demanded the man who was standing in front of the building.

"I am Captain Mossman of the Arizona Rangers. I have a letter from Judge Barnes for you."

After discussing the letter, Alvord stated he would have to solicit the help of Billy Stiles

in the matter. Mossman told him it was a good idea, and that he would place their names on the roster of rangers for the time being, as it would help with the promised pardon.

When Mossman returned home, he learned that President Theodore Roosevelt had appointed Major Brodie territorial governor of Arizona. This meant that Burt would probably have to resign as a ranger, since each new governor brought in his own people. To sidestep this possibility so that he could still work on the Chacon case, Mossman asked and received a deputy United States marshal commission from Marshal McCord at Phoenix. On September 1, 1902, Captain Tom Rynning replaced Mossman as head of the Arizona Rangers.

Finally, Billy Stiles contacted Mossman.

"Chacon and Alvord are camped in the San Jose Mountains near Naco; I'm to accompany you."

When they came near the outlaw camp, Alvord was seen riding toward them.

"I'm going for some whiskey," he said. And as he passed Mossman, he whispered hastily, "Watch out for Stiles, he'll double-cross you."

Chacon was seated alone next to the fire when Mossman and Stiles rode into camp. Stiles pointed to Burt, telling Chacon this was a new riding partner. Burt understood the hidden meaning and acted accordingly. He pretended to toss a cigarette into the fire, then quickly turned, revolver in hand, hammer back.

"Hands up, Chacon, and you too, damn you, Stiles!" cried Mossman.

Stiles paled. He had planned to rescue his friend Chacon.

"What in hell is the meaning of this, Mossman?" demanded Stiles.

"You know what I mean. Now get those cuffs out of your pocket and put them on your Mexican friend. I know you meant them for me, so move."

Mossman tied both men to their saddles, doubly insuring against the escape of Chacon by also throwing a loop over his head.

Several miles north of Naco, Mossman cut a wire fence and crossed the border. At the railroad junction stop at Packard, Mossman

Courtesy Mrs. James Risely

This handsome, beautifully-engraved, pearl-handled revolver was presented to Burton C. Mossman upon his retirement from the Arizona Rangers.

boarded the train with his prisoner, sending Stiles back to Bisbee with the horses.

"Dammit, Mossman, I thought sure you meant to take me in."

"Just wanted to make sure I got Chacon. Now get, and keep your damned mouth shut about this. If I were you, I'd make myself scarce around Arizona."

Mossman realized that Chacon was waiting his chance to escape, and he was worried. However, at Benson they had a chance meeting with sheriff Parks of Graham County, who had taken some prisoners to Yuma. He had his leg and arm irons, so now Chacon was securely shackled and his doom was sealed.

When Chacon appeared before the judge at Solomonville, Mossman was afraid positive identification of the prisoner would be lacking. But the Mexican took care of that when he said, "Yes, I am Chacon, and am not afraid to die."

His friends hired lawyers in an effort to prove that Chacon was kidnapped form Mexican soil, but try as they might, they could not find the two principal witnessess, Stiles

and Mossman. Stiles had taken Burt's advice and disappeared. Mossman was enjoying life in New York City on November 23, when Chacon dropped through the trap door on the scaffold.

Billy Stiles escaped the territory and went to China for a time. Later, he returned to the United States and lived in Nevada under an alias. He was killed by a young boy who shot him off his horse with a load of buckshot. Stiles had been a deputy at the time and had killed the boy's father when the man resisted arrest. Many believed that Alvord was able finally to dig up his stolen gold and to live in comfort the rest of his days in Panama.

As for Burton Mossman, his work was done in Arizona. He went to the Pecos country of New Mexico for his final move. Mossman had married Grace Coburn in Kansas City on December 12, 1905. A son, Burton, Jr., but always called "Billy," was their first child. In 1909 a second child was born, a girl called Mary. But a terrible blow struck Mossman nine days later when Mrs. Mossman passed away. Another tragedy struck the grand old man when his son, Maj. Billy Mossman, was killed in 1943 when his plane was shot down during World War II.

In 1944, the remains of the Diamond A Ranch were sold, and Mossman settled down to enjoy the rest of his life with his second wife, the charming Ruth Shrader, whom he had married in 1925.

The savior of Arizona, as he had become known, and first captain of the Arizona Rangers died at Roswell, New Mexico, on September 5, 1956, and was buried in the Mount Washington Cemetery at Kansas City, Missouri.

Chapter Nine

Tom Vernon, Tragedy on the Sweetwater

MANY A young TV viewer today concocts a gruesome daydream as he wonders how much hardship he could have stood if he had lived in the days of the Indian frontier battles. But no such daydream has ever equaled the true experience of Buffalo Tom. I knew Tom well in his later years, and he explained to me his train robbery experience of 1928, when he tried to hold up the Union Pacific train at Archer, Wyoming. He also told me of his prison experiences, as well as giving me photos and notes dealing with his Sweetwater days. This is Tom's story.

This was the boy who was exposed to murder by supposedly civilized white men and miraculously saved by supposedly savage Sioux Indians in the Dakotas. Tom Averill grew up to become famous as Buffalo Tom Vernon, the buffalo rider in the wild west shows staged throughout the world by Buffalo Bill Cody.

Knowing that his life story was too fabulous to be easily believed, Tom went to considerable trouble to document his claims regarding his birth and the death of his parents. It was his aim in life to vindicate his mother and father from the false and scandalous reports which the cattle barons spread in their campaign to sweep the plains of homesteaders, so as to keep the range open for their own purposes.

And, Tom succeeded in correcting the record. He even left to posterity a list of names of the Wyoming cattle syndicate members who had engaged the killers to do their bloody work.

Until Tom was eight years old, he lived in a neat little log cabin behind a general store which his father, Jim Averill, had established on the Old Oregon Trail near Independence Rock, in Carbon County, Wyoming. He played in the lush bottomlands of the Sweetwater River and thought that life was wonderful on the green prairie where his parents had each homesteaded one hundred sixty acres.

His mother, Ella Averill, the daughter of Missouri and Kansas pioneers, had the pluck of the best pioneer women. She labored beside her husband to improve their home year by year.

They raised vegetables and cows and horses. The haphazard business at their store developed more and more as numerous homesteaders moved into the region. It looked to the Averills as though their hard work had put them on the road to success, and all their neighbors within a radius of fifty miles respected them for their fortitude.

But the range had previously been open to the roaming cattle of the big outfits. Now, as each homesteader fenced his one hundred sixty acres to meet the government's requirements, he was marked as an enemy. Enough homesteaders and enough fences would ruin the business of the cattle barons. Ruthlessly, they undertook to discourage the settlers.

There was only one way of preventing new pioneers from staking claim to the land: frightening the homesteaders already there into leaving, and making it clear to others that the dangers were too great to surmount.

It was not difficult to hire men without scruples who would, for a price, carry out a campaign of threat. Nevertheless, the threats did not intimidate the hardy settlers. Then it was that the organized cattlemen resorted to tangible harm, creating horrible examples of what awaited any settlers who dared to enter the region.

Tom was not too young to sense the grip of fear as various settlers stopped at the general store, which was also a post office, to make purchases and confided their troubles to Jim and Ella Averill. He listened with the same dramatic suspense that a boy of today watches a TV story about cowboys beating rustlers to the draw. It was exciting, but it seemed far away from reality, and Tom did not take it seriously for a long time.

Finally, however, even a boy of eight could not ignore the evil undertones, especially when threats were fulfilled with murder and ruin. When one after another homesteader had been threatened with death if he did not move westward, and later had been found dead in a gulley, nobody could consider such a string of disasters as isolated incidents. The homesteaders soon realized that a systematic campaign was directed against them, and that none of them was exempt from the attacks of the powerful combination.

The crime of the settlers was their making use of a part of the range which the cattlemen were determined to keep for themselves.

Regardless of government approval of their claims, regardless of the hardships by which they had paid for their one hundred sixty acres apiece, their rights as landowners on the prairie were never to be respected by the big cattle owners.

Whenever Tom heard about fences torn down and cattle driven off to places where they were never seen again, he felt defiant and wanted to take revenge. Constantly, he heard about whole wheat fields or barley fields that were burned in the night. Barns and dwelling

Carl Breihan Collection

Buffalo Tom Vernon Averill gained fame as a rider with Buffalo Bill's world-known Wild West Show. His life's story was most unusual, even for the Old West.

places were repeatedly left in ashes. In order to save their lives, the settlers had to flee.

Gradually, Tom was consumed with fear and furious anger at the same time. One of the reasons for this complex of emotions was his helplessness to do anything to correct the injustice. Even the grownups failed in all their efforts to forestall the arson and the murder.

Jim and Ella (Watson) Averill steadfastly refused to run when they were threatened, and Tom looked upon them with wonder at their courage.

Jim Averill was a short, thick-set man who relied upon his own integrity and who, even when recognizing the danger which hovered over the whole region, believed he could win out against the crooks. His wife stood beside him and practically stiffened his spine by her own braveness. Tom's fear almost evaporated when he saw his parents refusing to join settlers who left in their last wagons. He admired the way they stood by their rights, ready to face whatever battles they had to fight in order to protect their homestead.

Jim Averill, a graduate of Cornell University, was a well-read man, and one of the reasons that the cattle barons first marked him as a danger to their plans was that he had read and digested the laws which defined the rights of the homesteaders. The crooks could frighten men who were not entirely sure of their legal rights, but Jim Averill could answer them back by quoting a pertinent section of the Wyoming code.

Worst of all, Jim Averill subscribed to eastern newspapers. He read the false reports which the big cattlemen spread against the homesteaders. According to them, every settler was a thief and a liar. In turn, Jim Averill wrote to the newspapers a correction of the false reports, explaining the case for the homesteaders, and his letters were printed in the same columns. In 1888, he also sent such a letter to the Casper, Wyoming, *Daily Mail.*

However, his feeble voice was not equal to the organized campaign in the newspapers. It was merely accepted by the citizens in Wyoming as a warning that Averill was a man they had to blot out. They recognized him as the spearhead of the opposition to their unjust monopoly of the land.

The homesteaders were acquainted with the Board of Livestock Commissioners, who were always finding some excuse to prove that their fences were in the wrong place or that they had not legally proved-up on their claims. Even though they had government papers to back up their claims, they were constantly flouted.

There was another organization called the Cattlemen's Association, but this was composed of the same men who made up the membership of the Board of Livestock Commissioners. First, one group claiming to be from one "official" combination and then another group claiming to be from the other would ride up to a ranch and demand what they called their rights. The average settler was completely confused by the "legal" accusations hurled at him, and if he held out for awhile, it was only to meet more deadly measures.

After their threats, the cattlemen sent their hired gunmen to use fire as a persuasion that a settler had better not stay. If the burning of all his possessions did not convince him, then he was shot when he went to round up his cattle. Widows and children after such episodes usually found some way of getting off the prairie, but it did not matter to the big outfits where they went to or how. Their whole object was to clear the prairie, so that their cattle could roam on a never-ending pasture.

One "accident" after another made the prairie a hell of fear, and no man with a family dared to risk their welfare. Family after family withdrew toward the west, hoping to find government protection in some spot not being stifled by the big cattlemen.

Jim Averill decided that the homesteaders ought to organize for their own protection against the Board of Livestock Commissioners and the Cattlemen's Association, so one day he called a meeting in his trailside store. Settlers from many miles around came to discuss ways in which they could get government protection or in which they could help one another to continue on their claims. But the only result of this meeting was that Jim Averill

Buffalo Bill Cody (right) and Pawnee Bill Lillie came
to Tom Vernon's aid, and attested to his true identity.
He went to considerable trouble to prove who he was.
He saw his parents hanged by renegades.

Tom Vernon as he appeared when riding with Buffalo Bill's great
western show.

became more-than-ever a marked target for
the barbs of the syndicate.

The settlers had brought their families
through hundreds of miles on starvation
rations. They had fought Indians and had seen
their loved ones die of wounds or sickness
before they arrived at their destination. They
had continued to starve and had worked with
superhuman zest in order to prove up on their
acres. Moreover, they were still without com-
forts and still lacked bare necessities. But they
were willing to hang on, through natural
miseries, in the hope of eventual success.

However, to live through evil attacks by
men determined that they should never enjoy
the land on which they labored, regardless of
their legal rights, sickened them. For a piece
of their own land, they were willing to suffer,
but against the "bloated octopus" of their organized enemies, they chose to flee.

Despite (even because of) Jim Averill's newspaper letters, and despite his letters to the
land office in Washington, the situation became more and more desperate. After all, near
neighbors had been burned out or shot, one
family after another had been glad to get away
in a bare wagon after their other possession
had been destroyed, the Averills still held out.
But they felt the pressure increasing as one
effort after another was made to catch them
in a position that would justify one of the
gangsters into killing them or in dragging
them off to jail.

Once a stranger was brought into the store
by Black Mike, a man in the employ of the
cattlemen. The stranger had been told that
Ella Averill was Cattle Kate, a rustler and
woman of loose morals. He made advances
toward her which might have been calculated
to inspire Jim Averill to start shooting. Jim
himself would then have been shot from be-

hind, the blame left upon him for having drawn first. But in this instance, Jim beat the stranger with his bare hands and thus got rid of him.

Another time, Black Mike tried to encourage Jim to sell whiskey to an Indian. That would have been an excuse to march Averill off to jail.

Tom saw one family after another come by to explain their going.

"They've burned me flat," they all said. "Just before dawn, fire started in the barn and the house at the same time. It started from burning arrows shot into the hay and through the house windows. The fields are black now. You better get, Jim. They'll get you next."

"I'm staying," said Averill.

"We're staying," said Ella, standing beside her husband.

Tom wanted to go along with this last family, because without them, there would be no children for him to play with anymore. But he was thrilled at the heroism of his parents. Besides, he had a hazy idea that he might grow up in time to conquer the organized cattlemen before they could do much more damage.

As each family stopped at the store to say goodbye, Tom heard the half-hearted remark: "If any mail comes, save it till you hear where we're at."

None of the retreating families had any idea where they would go next, or what they would do. Simply, they could no longer buck the opposition of the cattlemen. Each time, Ella Averill went out to the wagons to talk with the women, they were all crying. They had begun to be afraid they would never find a place of safety.

Tom watched as his parents bade farewell to all the families which ringed the store in a radius of fifty miles. Now at last, the Averills were alone, their only hope of any communication with human beings lying in the trail by which travelers would be likely to pass.

What Tom as a little boy could hardly understand was the cruelest part of the enemy campaign; they had taken to smudging cattle brands and claiming that the homesteaders had rustled their cattle. Accusing them of being rustlers was the worst threat of all. Whenever a man was shot from behind, the cattlemen could always say he had been caught rustling and had run when accosted. No other explanation was necessary, and no defense could be procured.

Jim Averill said, "I'll see that they don't plant any blotched brands on me. I've got eighty cows and twenty head of horse, right branded and registered, and everybody knows what I got. I'll ride fence every day if I have to."

The next news to come was that Jim and Ella Averill had been reported as outlaws. The claim was that they had made a deal with a tribe of Indians and had been driving stolen cattle by the hundreds to the Dakotas. Jim Averill considered this with a determination to find a way to clear his name, but when he heard that it was rumored he and Ella had never been married, then his anger did flare.

"They better stay off that tack!" he shouted.

But he could not name the "they" and he could not shoot or strangle a gang of mysterious accusers.

Next, there was a night fire in the store, most accidental, of course, though Jim Averill found that a kerosene-soaked rag had started it, while he and his wife and son were asleep. He decided not to make any accusation, since he could not name the arsonist. But he had heard the flames crackling in time to rise and save the barn, and as soon as possible, he rebuilt the store and the hut in which the family made their living quarters.

When settlers rode over to help, Jim Averill said carefully, "Must have been a faulty flue."

One of the ranchers said, "Yeah, I've done a pile of traveling before I hit the Sweetwater. And I heard a lot about them bad flues all the way." Then he swung into the saddle and added, "There's gunna be a powerful lot o' bad flues from here on. You guys got my sympathy."

The next thing that happened was the loss of Jim's eighty cows through a cut fence, though that fence had been whole the day before. He trailed them to a gully where he found the eighty of them shot dead.

Jim kept his horses close to the barn after

Mr Tom Averill Vernon.
Major. G. W. Lillie.
Pawnee. Oklahoma.

Dear Tom;

It was a grate surprise to me when I open your letter. Dated Nov. 17th. from Cheyenne. it was the first word I have had of you after you left the 101 Ranch show. at Madson Squar Garden New York in May 1914.

It don my heart good to read your letter. knowing your Father Jim Averill and your Mother Ella. like I did and the cowderly way they were murder. and as I recall the hardship rendered against you as a child. it makes me feal as tho I should strap on my trusty old gun and help you run to earth those that have hounded you through your past life.

Tom. I was Riding for the U. T. Ranch. owned by the Durbin Brother's. at Split Rock Wyoming. at the very time your Parents were lynch. becaus they were Homesteders and some of the Boys from this Ranch found your Parents and maid the report. But we were on able to find you. and not untill Jim Mitchel came to old Fort Fittmer. Wyoming with White Eagle. a Chief from the Oglalas. did we lern as to your wharabouts.

I left the old U. T. Ranch. and returned to Pine Ridge. S. D. with Mitchel White Eagle and American Horse. I wanted to be sure you were safe. Major Gallagher the Agent at Pine Ridge. and Rock Bear. told how and whar you were found. and that Doctor Glennan. of the Eight's U.S. ... had probed a bullet out of your throught. whar you ... by some of the same one's that had murder ...

... to Major Lillie. and ... me again soon.

...ood Friend.

Tom C. Grant
Old Silver Tip.
Deadwood. S. D.

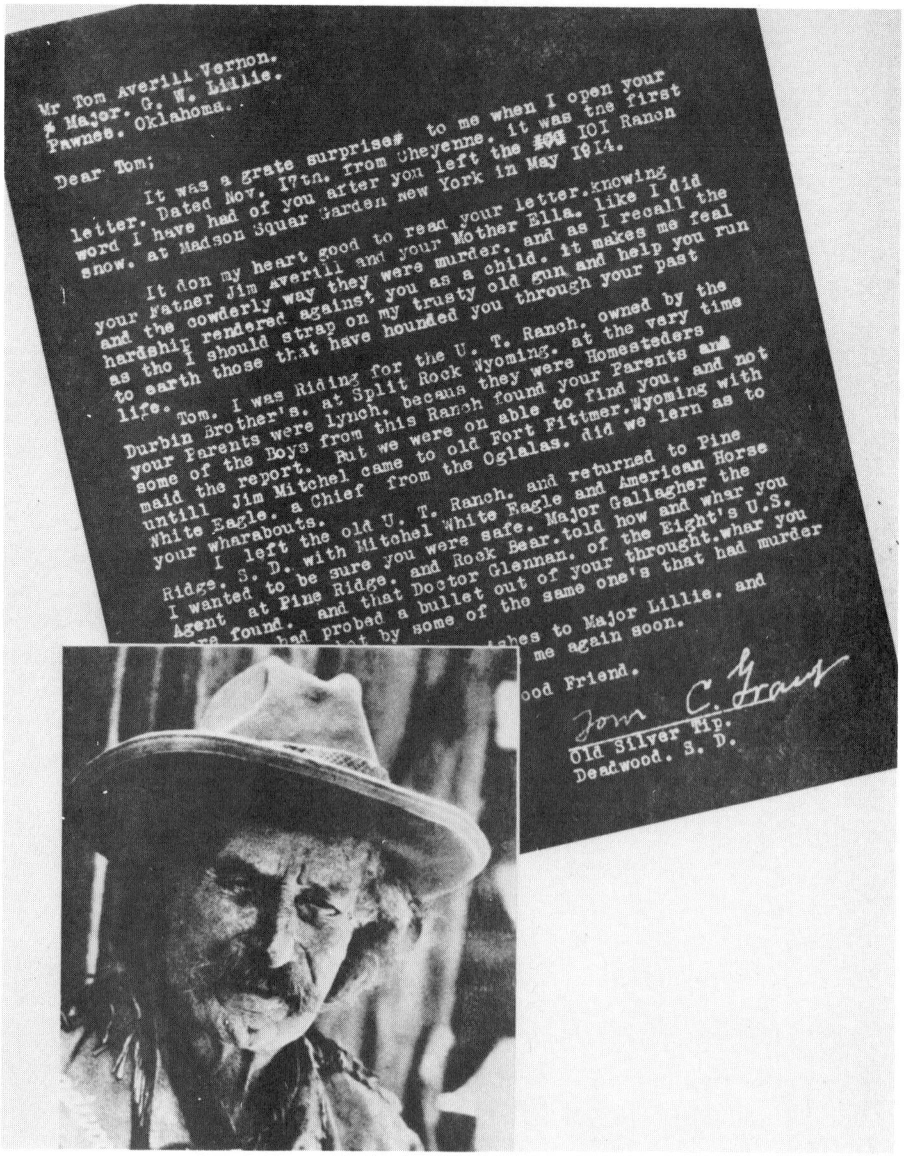

Carl Breihan Collection

Tom C. Grant, a neighbor of Jim Averill (Tom's father), was among those joining a posse to run down rustlers and killers. Known as "Old Silver Tip," he helped confirm Tom Vernon Averill's story with accompanying letter, shown here.

that, feeding them the hay that should have been kept for the winter. He never let himself sleep at night, but roamed about with his rifle, doing all he could to protect his place. But the rumors continued, and the thing Jim Averill suffered most about was the tale spreading that his wife was Cattle Kate, a rustler and bawdy woman. There was no way he could fight back.

One day a dust cloud in the distance turned out to have been made by seven riders, booted and spurred, wearing leather chaps and flat-crowned hats tied under their chins. These were no ordinary cowboys, but strangers brought to the prairie on salary from the cattlemen. And today, their leader was Black Mike, the most notorious of all the hired thugs.

They came raging into the store, and Black Mike said, "We give you warning enough, Averill. So now we've come to arrest you for rustling and for blotching brands and running other people's stock into the Dakotas. We're the law."

"Law, nothing," said Averill.

But the men forced Jim and his wife into a waiting wagon, the men telling the pair they were being taken to Rawlins. When young Tom tried to defend his parents by kicking and biting at the men, he was kicked aside. Through dirt and tears, he saw Black Mike reach for him, and grab him by the collar. Kicking and screaming, Tom was tossed across Black Mike's saddle and pressed against the horn, the wind jolted out of him. He was roped and forced to ride along with the marauders after they clattered out of the store. Jim and Kate did not appear to be frightened as much as the men would have liked, as they taunted and laughed at the grim-faced riders.

Near the mouth of a small canyon, the two condemned parties were forced to alight from the wagon and to walk to a large cotton wood tree on the Sweetwater.

"Put the prisoners on horses," commanded Black Mike.

This done, nooses were placed over Jim and Ella's heads. Even to this point, Averill thought it was all a joke. The men hadn't even bound their hands together; it was an amateur group who hadn't thought of it. The ropes hissed over a stout branch of the cottonwood, the loose ends tied securely to the base of the tree.

"My God!" cried Averill. "You men aren't serious about this?"

Black Mike laughed out loud, "Ladies first."

"No use hanging a woman, kill me if you like, but let Ella go," pleaded Averill.

"She's in this as deep as you are. And after you two, we'll take your young whelp and swing him by the fetlocks and bash his head on a wagon hub. That'll get rid of the whole layout. Ain't leavin' no whelps in this coyote den."

At this Tom's mother let out a piercing scream.

"Slap those horses and let 'em swing," Black Mike ordered.

As both horses leaped forward, Jim and Ella swung into space. It took them a long time to die, since it was strangulation that killed them and not the customary broken necks in a regular hanging. Young Tom looked on in frenzy as he saw his parents struggling, their eyes bulging in their sockets, bloody foam dripping from their mouths.

"Dad! Dad!" the boy cried, but he was completely helpless.

Black Mike heaved a fist at him and he landed against a tree trunk yards away. When he was able to open his eyes, he saw his parents still swinging in the slight breeze, their bodies now motionless in death . . . it was summer, 1889.

When Black Mike was sure Ella and Jim were dead, he turned to young Tom. Despite Tom's kicking and screaming, Black Mike got him by the shoulders, then swung him upside down, seizing his ankles. He swung the boy like a pendulum, and Tom was no longer able even to scream. He felt himself giddying back, aimed at a tree trunk, and he knew his head was about to be bashed.

But suddenly two hands caught at Tom's shoulders in the middle of the final swing.

"Let go, Mike. I don't go for kid killing," cried one of the men.

Tom was almost out of his mind. He had given himself up and by now had lost all sense of hope. But he heard what the men were saying about his parents, "Leave 'em for the buzzards."

Black Mike was still arguing about Tom, "He's a witness. What yo' gonna do with 'im?"

"We'll ditch 'im when we get to the Dakotas," said the other man. "Let the Injuns find him. It's their funeral what they do with 'im."

Tom was then hoisted to the saddle in front of the man who had saved him, and he was almost too numb from pain and anger to think straight. He was frozen silent, but he was shivering so that he could hardly sit on the front of the saddle.

The men took him back to his parents' home and held him by a rope while they looted the place. In the barn, they caught his own pony and tied him to the saddle. In the meantime, he watched the men opening his father's stock of whiskey and gulping down the stuff as they packed as much of the other merchandise as they could into their saddle bags. And then he saw them set fire to the store and the barn.

The group moved on, Tom on his pony, dragged by a rope which one of the riders held. All he knew now was that they were headed for Dakota where they would throw him to the Indians. He was beyond fear for the time being, almost crazy with grief and horror. The blows he had received were so painful that several times he blacked out.

But he was dragged along, and the men made camp twice before they spotted a dugout with a rotted long roof.

"Here's a good place to leave the runt!" cried one of them.

They talked about the nearby Indian tracks and decided that the boy might be found sooner or later, if they left him here.

Black Mike, however, insisted on tying Tom inside the dugout with a piece of chain and some wire to make it impossible for him to escape by himself. When Tom was secured and the riders had left, he tried to muster up the strength to call for help, when he saw Black Mike sneak back to the dugout and grin at him.

Black Mike aimed his gun and fired.

In the dugout, the explosion roared, and Tom felt hot pain in his throat. He blacked out for many hours.

When he regained consciousness, his feet and legs were stiff and he was shivering in the cold dark. He tried to stir. At the rattle of the chain, he suddenly remembered the whole terror, while pangs shot through his body, and the pain in his jaw and throat seemed unbearable.

Despite the pain, he tried to shout. He yelled at intervals, every time he could make himself brave enough to stand the pain caused using his throat.

After daylight had seeped into the dugout, he heard what may have been a footstep, or it may have been only the snapping of a twig. He was afraid it meant the approach of some wild animal, and new terror rose.

But in the full flood of sunlight he made out the head and shoulders of a human being slowly crouching to look at him. Evidently, his weak shouts had been heard.

At last, he saw that the head had a ragged scalplock from which hung a single eagle's feather. The face beneath it was streaked with white and vermillion paint. Tom's terror mounted.

Without realizing what he was doing, he felt that he ought to run, unreasonable though that was. And the slightest movement of his limbs made the chain rattle. Evidently that frightened the Indian. At any rate, the head and shoulders disappeared. Tom lay in a rigid silence, and minutes later, the Indian returned.

Tom saw the Indian creeping toward him. He held his breath in the worst fear yet.

The Indian inspected carefully the way Tom was tied. After working over the wire with his teeth and his fingers, at last he was able to free the boy. He carried Tom into the sunlight and unfastened the thong on his wrists. He tried to get Tom to stand, but Tom fell in pain and exhaustion.

Therefore, the Indian carried him against his musky brown hide, and for the first time, Tom realized that he was safer with this native than he had been with the white men.

When Tom saw the hides stretched between the tepees on poles, he knew that he was in a Sioux hunting camp. He saw brown children and square-faced women gather around to peer down at him. He was placed on a hide on the ground. A band of braves came running to inspect him, and their leader was wearing an embroidered vest.

This leader attempted to say some words in English, and though Tom could hardly make his sore mouth speak, he managed to say, "Black Mike shot me."

Inquiringly, the Indian pantomined the shooting of a rifle, and Tom nodded.

A buxom native lifted Tom in her arms, carried him into a tent, and placed him on a mat of buffalo skins. She bathed the gunshot wound in his neck and crooned over him. Then she placed hot poultices on his jaw, and he felt soothed by the fragrance of herbs.

A few days later, the Indians managed to call Dr. Glennan from the United States Eighth Cavalry. Gradually, Tom grew stronger under Dr. Glennan's care and under the loving ministrations of Morg, the woman. He learned that the Indian in the beaded vest was Chief Iron Tail, and that the one who had found him in the dugout was called White Eagle.

Dr. Glennan explained that it was necessary for him to remove the bullet from the back of Tom's neck, where it had lodged after striking his jaw. This was evidently such a painful operation that Tom never afterward remembered it. He probably blacked out while Dr. Glennan was working on him.

Dr. Glennan had the idea that if the man who had shot Tom ever heard that the boy was alive, he might come back to kill him. Therefore, he cautioned the Sioux to guard Tom carefully.

Everybody seemed to doubt that Tom could have come from such a faraway place as Sweetwater, and he did not have enough strength to insist. Actually, he was unable to talk to anybody about the horror he had witnessed. Whenever he was questioned, he found it impossible to force his lips to report all that had driven him nearly out of his mind.

Tom regained his strength and learned to like the Indian children, who played with him and told him the Indian names for things. Within six months, he was as tanned as his playmates, and as wild as they. One day when he seemed to have completely forgotten the old terror, he saw his playmates disperse like quail and disappear in the undergrowth along a stream. But We-No-Na, and Indian girl, grabbed him by the wrist and tried to drag him to safety.

She shrieked like a screech owl, just as Black Mike dismounted and grabbed the rawhide band around Tom's waist. He tossed Tom across his saddle and put his foot into the stirrup to remount. Tom sank his teeth into Black Mike's hand and started to kick. During the renewed screeching of the children, and while Tom was fighting furiously, Black Mike heaved himself into the saddle.

Suddenly, a husky voice cried, "Let him go!"

Black Mike started to grab his whip. But an Indian named Pete hurled himself from his own pony and with one arm around Black Mike's neck, dragged the desperate killer off his horse.

Tom, too, tumbled off and rolled over and over until he was out of the way of the hooves.

Then, Tom saw Black Mike fighting for his life; Pete clung to him and slowly choked him to death. They rolled about in the struggle, while Black Mike tried to get his spurs into Pete's legs. But Pete's wiry legs hugged Black

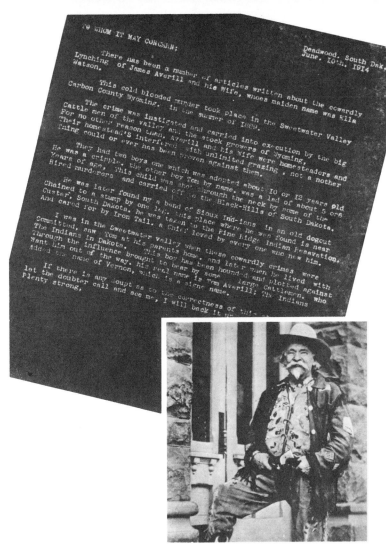

Carl Breihan Collection

Deadwood Dick Clarke confirmed what he described as "the cowardly lynching of Jim Averill and his wife," in the Sweetwater Valley in 1889. Clarke's signed statement blamed valley cattlemen and Wyoming stock growers.

Mike's abdomen like a strand of steel while his hands were relentlessly at his throat. It seemed an age to Tom before Black Mike lost his strength. His eyes popped out and his mouth sagged with his thick swollen tongue bleeding in streams through his teeth.

At last, Tom saw the final quiver in the legs of that hated Black Mike and the last stiffening tremor of his arms. Pete slowly released himself from the heavy carcass, and by that time, other Indians had arrived on their swift horses in answer to the screams of the children.

The whole Indian village rejoiced savagely for Tom's sake, for by now he was one of them. He grew up among them, learning from them to ride so well that he seemed to be part of his horse. They taught him also to make a lariat "talk," and for miles around he was known for his exceptional skill in training wild horses.

When Buffalo Bill Cody was preparing one of his wild west shows, he engaged one hundred Sioux as well as Tom to put on an act. But Tom was only fifteen years old at that time, and it was necessary for Buffalo Bill to contract him through a legal guardian. The star of his show, the famous crackshot Annie Oakley, volunteered for that task. She was Tom's guardian until he reached the age of twenty-one.

As soon as he reached his manhood, Tom established his identity. He learned, among other things, that after he had been carried away from the cottonwoods where his parents had been lynched, cowboys had reported about the burning of Averill's store. The bodies of the Averills were found on Monday following the awful crime by a party of settlers headed by Tom C. Grant, who was known as "Silver Tip." Jim Averill was given a decent burial, and the body of Ella Averill was claimed by her father, Thomas Watson of Rawlins, Wyoming. He learned also that six of the seven members of the lynch mob had been arrested after being identified by Frank Buchanan, Av-

erill's foreman. Buchanan had been a witness to the lynching, but had been unable to assist, since he was alone. Before the accused could be brought to trial, however, Buchanan was shot and killed from ambush. With the only witness gone, the case against the six was dropped by the court.

But they had long puzzled as to the fate of Tom . . .

When Tom was famous as Buffalo Tom Vernon, appearing in Madison Square Garden and many points west, he made public the names of the cattlemen who had hired Black Mike and the other marauders. There was little satisfaction in this, since none of them was ever punished. In fact, some of them had amassed fortunes as members of the guilty syndicate, and they had left riches to their kin. But the pioneers who had laboriously proved up on claims had been left impoverished, with nothing to bequeath to their own loved ones.

Nevertheless, the record stands. The only survivor of the Sweetwater Massacre was at least worthy of his brave parents in his own courage and skill. He long performed throughout the country as a buffalo rider and a trainer of wild horses.

Never has a TV thriller equaled the actual experiences of Tom Vernon.

Chapter Ten

Captain Jack Slade

IT HAD BEEN a hot day and Joseph (or Jack)* Slade was in a bad mood. As he stopped in the shade of the express stable, he dragged his Bull Durham and cigarette paper from his pocket to roll a cigarette. Suddenly he heard excited voices coming from the interior of the building. Ordinarily no eavesdropper, the tone of the conversation was of interest to Joe.

---

*Full name: Joseph Alfred Slade, born near Carlyle, Illinois, 1829.

"They tell me the bosses are hopping mad in not being able to get a new station agent at Julesburg. That old Frenchman, René Jules, has them buffaloed for good."

"I'd hate to mess with that damned killer," Jack heard further.

At that particular moment, he strolled casual-like into the stable, pretending not to have heard the conversation.

"Hello, boys! What a hot day. I'd sure like to shuck the dust off this place and head for cooler climate," Jack said.

Carl Breihan Collection
Joe (Jack) Slade was known as plenty tough, a skilled gunslinger. This is believed to be the only known likeness of him in existence.

"How about Colorado?" one of the men snickered. "It's cool up there."

"Sounds good. What's going on up there?"

"The company needs a new agent at Julesburg. Maybe you'd like to try for that."

"Why not?" was Jack's response, as he strolled from the stable.

Just as he suspected, the next morning he was called into the offices of Russell, Majors, and Waddell, operators of the Pony Express. Slade was awed by the ornate furnishings of the office, the deep pile rug, and the heavily carved desks and chairs which dotted the richly-furnished room.

"What's this I hear about you wanting to leave St. Joe?" Mr. Majors asked.

"Yep, always wanted to run a stage station of my own. How about letting me take over the Julesburg route?"

"Man, you crazy? Jules would make mincemeat out of you in no time," said Mr. Russell.

As it was, Jack Slade was a short, round-faced man with mild blue eyes and a pleasant personality. No wonder the bosses thought he was unfit for such a job.

"Well, I believe I can handle the job; besides, don't believe you got anybody else willing to try. I've killed several men and was just a short hop ahead of a posse from Illinois when I hit St. Joe."

Taken back by the nerve and audacity of this little man, Russell suggested that they give him a chance at the job.

"By the way, what's your name?" asked Majors.

"Jack Slade."

"All right, Jack, we'll write out Jules' dismissal papers and you can get started off right away. Come back in an hour or two, and we'll also clue you in as to the situation out there."

Later that day, Slade was informed by the owners how René Jules,* superintendent at Julesburg, was doing some freighting of his own. He was helping himself to the grain and hay purchased for the firm's horses and using company supplies to suit himself. The owners knew they were losing money at that station, but were afraid to cross the cruel Frenchman,

---

*Also Jules Reni

a burly, arrogant man, hated by everyone and feared for his vicious reputation.

The next morning Slade packed his scant belongings and, with Jules' discharge papers in his pocket, headed west on a company stage.

The wily ex-private** of the Mexican War liked the climate of Colorado and took the trip easily and uneventfully. At Julesburg, he swung down from the stage and stretched his legs. As he did so, the smirking Jules came swaggering toward the stage to look over the passengers. For some reason, he singled out Slade.

"And who might you be?"

"Captain Slade."

"Don't mean a damned thing to me. Let's see your ticket."

"Don't need a ticket. I'm stopping and staying right here."

"Yeah? Where are you really going?" demanded the Frenchman.

"Nowhere, but you are," replied Slade.

Slade handed the curious Frenchman his dismissal notice and as he read it, his eyes flashed fire.

"Hand over the company keys, Jules, and we'll check the stock. We'll start with those in the corral."

With a swift eye, Slade could easily see that Jules had altered the brand on the company stock, and had placed the animals in his own corral.

"We'll get those stolen horses out of your corral first, Jules, and put them where they belong," said Slade.

"No goddam shrimp like you is going to tell me what to do!" cried Jules, as he whirled about, his .44 revolver spewing lead. Slade took five slugs in the body, and it appeared as though his job as superintendent at Julesburg was over. Still on his feet, Slade staggered toward the express station, blood spurting from his wounds with every step he took.

"Fall, damn you, fall!" yelled Jules, but Slade staggered on.

Puzzled, Jules rushed to the station office,

**Enlisted Co. A, First Regiment, Illinois, May 4, 1847, age 18, Alton, Illinois. Discharged Alton, Illinois, October 16, 1848, from Co. A, first regiment of Illinois foot volunteers.

Entrepreneures William Russell, Alexander Majors, and William B. Waddell put together the world's greatest freighting enterprise across the plains. They first hired Jack Slade.

grabbed a shotgun and fired at Slade's back. The heavy buckshot brought Slade to the ground.

"That should do it," grinned Jules, not noticing that his victim still breathed.

"Put the son-of-a-bitch over there; then get a box and dump him in," Jules told his men.

Just then Slade raised himself on one elbow and said, as Jules stared, his mouth dropping open, "Not just yet, men. Damn you, Jules, I'll see you dead, and I'll nail one of your ears to the corral post and wear the other as a watch charm."

The awed Jules raised his revolver to put a finishing bullet through Slade's head. He changed his mind and muttered, "Hell, he'll be dead in a minute anyway; why waste a shot?"

Just then, the eastbound stage, filled with miners, yelling and whooping, pulled into Julesburg.

99

One of the men wanted to know the cause of the ruckus, and when told the story of Jules back-shooting, the irate miners wanted to hang the Frenchman on the spot.

Rough hands half-dragged, half-carried the struggling Jules to the corral gate, where a rope was thrown over the top railing, and a noose placed around his neck. A dozen willing hands seized the rope and jerked the writhing Frenchman into the air.

"Hold it, men!" cried a voice from the stage office. "Slade's still breathing, but I sure can't figure out how he's still alive."

The leader of the lynching party scratched his grizzled chin.

"Dammit, guess we'd best wait 'til Slade kicks the bucket before we hang this no-good bastard."

The men suddenly let go of the rope, and Jules buckled in the dust like a sack of meal thrown from a wagon. He lay gasping for air, his bravado all gone.

"Don't hang me, don't hang me," he pleaded. "Let me go and I'll get out of Colorado."

"Seeing as how Slade's still alive, we might as well let the stinking coyote go," suggested one of the men, a passenger named Ben Ficklin who also was superintendent of the line between Salt Lake City and Denver.

Jack Slade was taken east by stage, where doctors removed most of the lead from his body, but some of it remained until the day he died. Slade was a tough character and survived the wounds inflicted by René Jules at Julesburg, Colorado.

It was months before he returned to that station and became known as "Slade of the Overland." Most people considered him a dangerous man — a man too tough to be killed by buckshot and bullets. All along the Pony Express route from St. Joe to Sacramento, Slade was talked about as an efficient and ruthless man.

There can be little doubt that he ran the station at Julesburg on a paying basis. Stages rolled in and out on schedule, and the equipment was kept in good order. Slade worked his men to a breaking point, but he got results. In that wild and desolate country, where fine horseflesh was an attraction for outlaws and rustlers, little loss of animals was experienced by the station which Capt. Slade operated.

Late one evening, Slade and several of his men ran across two men who had Pony Express horses in their possession. Here, Captain Slade was the law, as there was no official lawman for hundreds of miles. To bring the culprits in would have posed a great problem for Slade.

"We'll just hang 'em at the first handy tree," he commented.

His men gasped, but said nothing. The two rustlers knew it would be useless to plead or argue with the unfeeling Slade. In an hour, their lifeless bodies were swaying in the night breeze, to become food for the buzzards the next day.

In 1861 when Mark Twain met Slade at Julesburg, he returned with the statement that he believed Captain Slade had already slain twenty-eight men.

In the spring of 1861, Slade learned that René Jules was still in the territory, and bragging that he was going to kill Slade the next time they met. Slade knew well that if they did meet, one of them would have to be killed. This did not suit his purpose, for he wanted to get back at the Frenchman for his treachery and for the misery he had suffered at his hands. He sent word to Jules that he still intended to cut off his ears if he ever ran across him. Captain Slade issued a reward notice that he would pay five hundred dollars for René Jules brought in alive, not a dime if brought in dead.

Several days later, a party of Slade's men informed him they had located the Frenchman.

"Bring the son-of-a-bitch in any way you can, but don't harm him," Slade ordered.

In a matter of hours the news arrived that Jules was a captive at the next relay station; that he had been captured without a struggle. Slade was soon riding for the relay station.

"Where is the dirty bastard?" rasped Slade, upon his arrival.

"Out in the corral."

Leaping from his horse, Slade raced for the corral, and sure enough, there stood Jules, securely tied to a post. It was the first time they had seen each other since Jules had ordered his men to bury Slade.

"I'm a man of my word, Jules. I'm going to return some of the lead you poured into me, and then I'm going to cut off your damned ears."

Slade's hands snaked to his holsters and his guns leaped into his hands. Jules gasped in anticipation of getting a slug in his belly. None came. Slade slowly lowered the guns and watched in unholy glee as Jules squirmed. Jack repeatedly drew his pistols and lowered them without firing a shot. Soon he tired of seeing Jules suffer in this manner, so he began using his victim for a target. Slade's bullets nicked Jules in many spots without hitting a vital one. All over his body flesh had been gouged off enough to sting and to draw blood. Slade played with Jules like a cat with a mouse. Jules knew that to plead for mercy would be useless. He waited and perhaps even prayed that the next shot would be the last one.

"How do you like it?" asked Slade.

Jules did not reply . . . what would be the use?

René Jules now was a mass of bleeding, quivering flesh, a hideous thing, awesome to look upon. All of Slade's men had by now left the corral, too sick to stomach much more of this sadistic torturing. Yet they knew better than to interfere. It soon began to tell on Slade, too, for his face began to change to a chalk white, and his step became unsteady. Quickly he took aim and placed a last slug through Jules' head. The bloody figure of the Frenchman sagged against the ropes which held him. Slade then walked up to the corpse, drew his Bowie knife, and slashed off Jules' ears. One he nailed to the corral post; the other he carried as a pocket piece, as he said he would.

Jack Slade had made good his threat, but his torture of Jules must have preyed heavily upon his mind, for he took to drinking and when drunk, became a vicious menace.

In 1862 the firm of Russell, Majors, and Waddell sold out to Ben Holladay, who was already carrying mail to remote outposts, and who had established branch lines off the main

This rough-and-ready foursome rode the famed Pony Express. Shown are: back, William Richardson (left), Johnny Frye; front, Charlie and Gus Cliff.

trunk. One of Holladay's first actions was to fire Slade.

"I'm sick and tired of Colorado anyhow," said Slade. "I'll start my own freighting business in Montana. I hear there's money to be made up there."

With Slade went his wife, Maria Virginia Slade, a former dance hall percentage girl, who was as nervy as she was beautiful. One time after Slade had been captured by a band of rustlers intent on giving him a taste of his own medicine by hanging, he asked that he be allowed to see his wife for a last farewell. Slade was locked in a log cabin, while a messenger went to get his wife.

Pretty Maria made herself friendly with the

The Pony Express stables still stand at St. Joseph, Missouri, and are a major tourist attraction. Slade helped run the Pony Express for the R., M., & W.

ringleader of the band, and he finally consented to allow her to see Slade alone.

"Don't be long, gal, we got a hangin' to get done with."

"Thank you, I won't."

Maria really fooled the leader, for he even failed to have her searched. Once inside the cabin, she wasted no time in getting pistols out of her clothing, like out of a hardware store. Before the startled outlaws knew what was going on, Slade and his wife lunged through the cabin doorway, their guns blazing. Maria leaped into the saddle of her horse, with Jack climbing up behind her. They made their escape before the outlaws could muster enough sense to follow.

In 1863 the Slades arrived in Alder Gulch, Montana, with their small freighting outfit. In Virginia City, one of the gulch boom towns, Slade tried to obtain lumber on credit from N. P. Langford (a member of the vigilantes) to build a house, corral, and stables.

"I don't know you, Captain Slade; why should I give you that much credit?"

"Damn you, Langford!" cried Slade. "I'm Captain Slade of the Overland, that's who I am!"

Langford shrugged his shoulders, still unimpressed and still refusing to give Slade the credit he wanted.

Several hours later, Slade ran across John Ely, whom he knew and who talked to Langford in his behalf. This assistance enabled Slade to start his freighting business, one which was to prove quite an asset.

Practically all the supplies used at the camp were brought from St. Louis, Missouri, by boat to Fort Benton on the Missouri River. From that point, wagons transported the supplies over the old military road, leading through Deer Lodge, Beaverhead, and into the Big Horn country. In 1863, the river fell so low that steamboats found it impossible to navigate farther upstream than to the mouth of the Milk River. This point lay several hundred miles below Fort Benton.

The steamboat captains dumped the supplies there, and all consignees were notified to pick up their own freight. No one was anxious to comply with this request, since both sides of the river below Fort Benton were swarming with hostile Indians. The Sioux held control of the south and the Blackfoot tribes held the land to the north. The people of

Virginia City were really in trouble. If the supplies did not arrive before the great snows fell, many of the citizens probably would starve to death. It was impossible to get to the outside world once the snows came. Men with freight wagons refused to go into the Indian-infested land. Another serious handicap was the fact that no wagon road had ever been broken between Benton and the Milk River.

"You'll never catch me going into that damned area," said one old miner. "No road is bad enough, let alone that and the Indians to fight."

Captain Slade overheard much of the conversation between the various miners and became quite disgusted with it all.

"What the hell's the matter with you white-livered cowards? Get me all the best bullwhackers you can find, and all the mule skinners, and I'll make the trip all right. I'll need some guides and riflemen as well."

Before long, a line of sturdy freight wagons and a group of determined men started on the dangerous trip from Virginia City to the mouth of the Milk River. The trip to Fort Benton was made without mishap, but from that point onward a new trail had to be cut out of the raw wilderness. Willing and capable hands made a road on which the heavy wagons could travel. Mile after mile, the caravan inched forward, always on the alert for hostile Indians. Strangely enough, not an Indian was sighted during the entire trip from Fort Benton to the spot where the supplies had been left by the steamboats.

Allowing the men and animals only a short rest period, Slade ordered the wagons to be loaded with all possible haste. The return trip must be made before the heavy snows fell. The return trip was not so easy. A number of times,

they were harassed by Indians who wanted to fight, but were unwilling to attack such a strong group. Quicksands at fords, blizzards, and snow caused other delays, but nothing could hold Jack Slade and his men.

"C'mon, men, give it all you've got!" he would tell them. "We've not got far now."

Unbelievable as it may seem, the tired caravan reached Alder Gulch on December 15, 1863, without losing a man or a pound of freight. To this day, many people of the area speak of this yet unmatched feat. Slade had brought in the supplies in as thorough a manner as he had disposed of Jules.

"By golly, Slade did it!" was the cry that echoed through the camps.

Captain Slade took advantage of his hour and strutted around Alder Gulch and the vari-

Without question, the most celebrated Pony Express rider was Buffalo Bill Cody, shown here in later years.

Carl Breihan Collection

Buffalo Bill carried this revolver.

R. Riss Collection

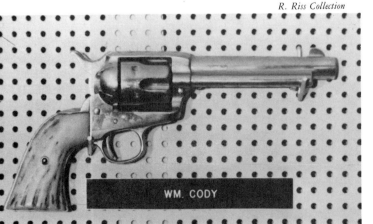

WM. CODY

ous camps as though he was a savior. In a way, he was. Anything Slade said was accepted as truth; anything he did was not questioned. Even when he raised hell while drunk, they said nothing. The citizens overlooked his faults because he had saved the camp from almost certain destruction.

With the profits realized from his daring overland venture, Slade invested in a hay ranch about eight miles from town. When the heavy snows prevented his freighting business from operation, Slade became fed up with nothing to do. He visited Virginia City quite frequently and raised Cain in the saloons with his old friends. He was a fiend when drunk. Jack would ride his horse into the saloons, wreck furniture, shoot up the place, and make a general nuisance of himself. Most everyone was happy when he left town to return to his ranch.

"You're carrying things too far, Slade," some of his friends warned him. "Keep this up and you'll end up on the noose end of a rope."

"Hell, man, they wouldn't do that to Slade; I saved the whole pack of them."

"That they know, and that is why you've gotten away with your cussedness this long. But don't say you weren't warned."

Several months after Slade's daring trip through the wilderness, the miners formed a vigilante committe to cope with the murders and robberies committed by an organized band. No town was spared the effects of these outlaws. Nevada City, Virginia City, and other camps in Alder Gulch were victims of their organized plans. The final results of the vigilante efforts to rid the territory of this menace was the capture and hanging of the Henry Plummer gang. Plummer was the pseudo-sheriff who killed and robbed by night, and acted as a peace officer during the day.

The vigilantes were in no mood to dicker with Slade. They had experienced a difficult time and were getting tired of Slade calling them "The Stranglers" and ridiculing them in public. Most of the miners remembered that Slade had performed them a great service, but even their patience was wearing thin.

"We're giving you another warning, Slade," he was told. "Your acts of violence cannot go unpunished forever."

But Slade refused to accept the warnings until it was too late. In March 1864, he appeared in Virginia City and met Bill Fairweather, one of the discoverers of Alder Gulch. The two were soon highly intoxicated and, surrounded by a bunch of drunken miners, they terrorized the town. Saloons and dance halls were taken over. The customers and dance girls were run out of the buildings. Next Jack led his drunken crew to the brothel house of Molly Featherlegs. He had been there once before and had wrecked the place, after which Molly warned him that if he returned, she would see that the vigilantes took care of him.

"Damn you, Jack Slade, get your drunken rabble out of my place!" she roared, as the men came stomping into her building.

"I want one of your women!" cried Slade.

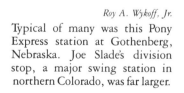

Roy A. Wykoff, Jr.
Typical of many was this Pony Express station at Gothenberg, Nebraska. Joe Slade's division stop, a major swing station in northern Colorado, was far larger.

W. F. Cody (Buffalo Bill), on the right, and Charles Cliff attended the 1912 dedication of this monument to the Pony Express at St. Joseph, Missouri. Both had been riders in their youth. Below are shown typical stamps. The Pony didn't last long, but is well-remembered.

"You'll get the vigilantes after this stunt," she warned.

"To hell with you and the damned vigilantes," replied the drunken Slade. "Let's have some music."

With that, he drew his revolvers and fired into the piano, wrecking it and sending the piano player diving for cover.

Molly dashed from the building and rushed to see Judge Alexander. She swore out a warrant against Slade. The judge attempted to appease the woman, but she refused to withdraw her demand.

"What the hell good did it do to hang Plummer and his gang, if you're gonna let Jack Slade shoot up the town and wreck any place he sees fit? Might as well let him rob us as to pay for the repairs. I want him arrested and made to pay for the damages."

Molly readily signed the affidavit, so the judge issued a warrant for Slade's arrest. She then returned to her establishment and informed Slade that she had filed charges against him.

"Damn you, woman, you'll regret this and so will those no-good vigilantes."

Slade then led his men on a rampage of terror which has never been equaled in Virginia City.

Acting Sheriff J. M. Fox finally located Slade and served him the warrant. Slade was ordered to appear before the people's court. He was in a jovial mood and agreed to accompany the sheriff. However, he did not go alone, for his drunken companions followed him. Judge Alexander read the warrant, charging Slade with malicious destruction of property and disturbing the peace. Slade's whiskey-hazed

105

mind went wild at that moment, and he seized the warrant from the judge's hand and tore it to bits.

"Here's what I think of your warrant!" he cried as he threw the bits of paper into the judge's face. Slade and his men then drew their revolvers and marched from the room.

Slade thought that his actions would go unpunished, just as those committed previously. But now many of the men who had taken their lives into their hands to bring law and order to the wild camps rebelled against Slade and felt that his wild actions should be punished or they would never cease. A meeting

was called and most of the leading men of Virginia City attended.

"Gentlemen," said Judge Alexander, "you know what has happened. If my court is to be placed in open defiance by Slade, then others will also try it, and the cause of the vigilantes has failed. Such actions can no longer be ignored. Yes, I know we all owe a lot to Slade, but I think he has over stepped his expectancy of gratitude."

As a result of this meeting, a message was sent to the miners in Nevada City, and a large body of them headed for Virginia City. All were armed and determined to stop once and

Walker-Missouri Commerce

This huge statue at St. Joseph, Missouri, depicts the dashing Pony Express rider carrying the mail over the plains to California, and return. The sculpture indicates also the romance involved, on a par with King Arthur's Knights of the Round Table.

106

for all the wild tactics of the drunken Slade and his men.

"You damned fool, Slade," his friends told him, "you just about sealed your own death warrant. You best leave for home and this may smooth over."

But he refused to listen, and nothing affected him until he learned that the people's court had condemned him and that his execution only awaited the arrival of the vigilantes from Alder Gulch. Slade agreed to leave town, but it was too late!

As Slade left the saloon, the vigilantes arrived to arrest him.

James Williams, the vigilante leader, read the decision: "The people's court agrees that Jack Slade shall die by hanging."

"You mean to hang me?" gasped the doomed man, hardly able to believe his ears.

"The people cannot stand it any longer, Slade. You had plenty of warning; you've no kick coming."

Finally, the message sank into his alcohol-dimmed brain. All Slade's bravado vanished. He wept, pleaded, and begged his captors to run him out of town, anything, but not to hang him. But all his pleas were ignored. The miners were determined to finish their task. It did not take long to drag the victim to the place of execution.

Slade's friends followed and made a feeble attempt to rescue him, but the vigilante guns held them at bay.

"Hang him at once, before his wife gets here," said one of the men. "Someone has sent word to her. We don't want to hang him in front of her."

Even as the man talked, Maria Virginia Slade was racing to her husband's side as fast as horseflesh could carry her. Someone saw her about a mile from town and gave the cry.

"Here comes Mrs. Slade; let's get this over with quick."

A large packing box was quickly placed under the gallows, and the condemned man hoisted upon this makeshift platform. Slade was in a state of collapse, so two miners supported him. Some later said they doubted that Slade actually knew what was going on, he

Denver Public Library, Western History Department
Virginia Slade was Jack Slade's wife, just as full of vigor and bold action as he. She bucked the Alder Gulch vigilantes and tried to stop his hanging, but arrived too late.

was in such a daze. Possibly, he was thinking of Jules and how he had tortured him.

"All right, men, let 'er go!" cried the leader, and the box was jerked from under Slade's feet. His neck was broken by the fall, and he died without a struggle.

Slade had scarcely passed into the beyond when his wife dashed upon the scene, her mount in a lather and ready to drop from exhaustion.

Maria threw herself upon Slade's body, weeping and cursing his slayers, until she was prevailed upon at last by friends to leave the scene.

"You dirty bunch of so-called vigilantes!" she cried. "You're all a bunch of lousy killers. You killed the man who saved the damned lot of you from starvation. He never killed or

Joe or Jack Slade's boyhood home was at Carlyle, Illinois. From this modest beginning, he wrote his name in western history with a sixgun and consistent brutality.

robbed anyone here. I'll not shame his body by burying it in Montana soil."

She was dead serious in her statement, for she had the blacksmith build a metal-lined box in which Jack's remains were placed. Ironically enough, she then filled the box with alcohol, the cause of Slade's whole trouble, and then sealed it to await burial.

Captain Slade was hanged on March 10, 1864, and months later, the stage road to Salt Lake City was opened for travel. Sometime in June, the Peabody & Caldwell stage pulled out of Virginia City for Utah, a distance of nearly five hundred miles. Inside the stage rode Mrs. Slade and her breed friend, Jimmy.

It was late in July when the stage rolled into Salt Lake City. At the depot, Mrs. Slade hired a wagon to take the sealed coffin to a local undertaker. When she had driven up to the building, the owner of the establishment walked out and addressed her, "What is it, ma'am?"

"I wish to bury my husband."

The man called his assistant and they lifted the crude coffin and carried it inside the building. As they pried off the lid, the room filled with alcohol fumes.

The undertaker and his aide gasped and backed off.

"What in thunder you got in there? Smells like an old still."

"Look inside," said Mrs. Slade.

Firmly holding their nostrils pinched closed, the two men peered into the box. Inside the container they saw a man's body, covered with alcohol, the neck bearing a swollen ring of bruised flesh.

"Who is this man?" gasped the undertaker, casting an anxious glance at his assistant.

"Jack Slade. He was hanged by vigilantes at Virginia City last March," came the simple reply.

The men's eyes popped.

"Jack Slade! Yes, we read about that and how his wife preserved the body in alcohol because she refused to allow his remains to be buried in Montana. Of course, we did not believe it at the time."

"Well, you can believe it now. Give him a decent burial and take it out of this money," said Mrs. Slade, as she turned and left the building.

The sexton's entry at the cemetery was a simple one. In his book of the City Cemetery burials appears: "Lot No. 6, grave 7, from

A rustic headstone marked the grave of Joseph Alfred Slade in the Salt Lake City Cemetery — block B, lot 6, grave 7. The stone was erroneously marked "I. A. Slade." Virginia Slade brought the body to Salt Lake, planned returning Slade to Illinois. But it never happened . . .

Bannack, Virginia City, Montana, J. A. Slade, buried July 20, 1864 on Lot B, single. To be removed to Illinois in the fall."

Of course, the removal never occurred; to this day Jack Slade lies in a grave in Salt Lake City, marked simply with VII. True, Joseph Alfred Slade had been born in Carlyle, Illinois, apparently in 1829, as his army enlistment papers read age 18 when he mustered in at Alton, Illinois on May 22, 1847. Jack's father, Charles W. Slade, came from Virginia in 1816 to Illinois, where he founded the present town of Carlyle. He was the congressman of that district in 1832, dying of cholera while en route from Washington, D.C. He was buried in the Carlyle Cemetery, where there are also several unmarked graves of the Slade family.

After the Civil War, Slade headed west, and it is doubtful if he ever again returned to Illinois. His birthplace was demolished in 1940. It should have been preserved as an historical landmark, but this tragedy has happened to so many old famous homes, and to me that is a pity.

True to another promise, Mrs. Slade never again lived in Montana. But in March of 1865, she returned to Virginia City to marry James H. Kiskadden. They returned to Salt Lake City, where they lived for nearly two years. Then the marriage broke up. Mrs. Slade obtained a divorce and headed east with her friend, Jimmy Sarah, and it was rumored that she either went to Denver or Chicago. The young breed named Sarah returned to his people in Wyoming.

Everyone in Montana had just about forgotten Jack Slade when a letter from a Chicago attorney, dated March 12, 1890, was received by the courts in Virginia City. The letter asked that any money remaining from the proceeds from the sale of Slade's property be forwarded to him. There should have been several thousand dollars or more from the sale of Slade's "Ravenwood Ranch" on the Madison River, and from the proceeds realized from his cattle and farm machinery, yet only several hundred dollars remained in the estate escrow when the attorney's request arrived. It is not known for sure if even that small amount ever reached Slade's widow.

James Kiskadden married again, this time to an actress named Annie Adams. To this marriage was born a girl who was destined to become the famous actress-headliner, Maude Adams.

Chapter Eleven

Hanging Judge Parker and George Maledon

HE WAS A LITTLE MAN, this George Maledon, standing only five feet five inches at full height; yet, as he worked his ropes with left-handed dexterity, the sight caused some command for respect. George was loved by his family, talked about by his friends, for his profession was one which did not appeal to all men. His deepset eyes and huge beard gave one the impression that he was devoid of any human feelings, especially when he was fondling his famous ropes.

At times, the little giant could be seen pacing back and forth on the scaffold platform, puffing away at his long German pipe, apparently trying to figure out a way to dispose of his victims in a quicker manner.

"The right and only humane way to hang a man is to break his neck instantly; that way they don't even twitch." This was his theory, and he worked at this matter until he had succeeded in perfecting a hangman's knot that did that very thing.

Maledon loved his ropes. They had to work to perfection at all times. He bought them in St. Louis, where they were woven from Kentucky hemp, soft and yielding, but strong enough to suit his purpose. George always ordered his ropes at one-and-one-eighth-inch thickness; then he would stretch them until they were only an inch thick. His indeed was a "labor of love," for he was paid only one hundred dollars for each hanging, minus funeral expenses for bodies not claimed by relatives. The eighty-seven men he sent to their deaths netted Maledon $8,700, less expenses, over a long period of years.

The hangman kept his ropes at home, where he would carefully oil them and make his hangman's noose, and when needed, the ropes were taken to the scaffold in a grocery basket. The scaffold where the executions were held, was built with a trap thirty inches wide and twenty feet in length, giving room for twelve men to stand thereon, side by side, at one time. Six men were executed at once on two occasions; three times, five were hanged together; as many times, four were executed at once, and on four occasions, three men were dropped off together, while double executions became too numerous to invite comment. When he left his gruesome occupation, Maledon took with him three ropes: one from which twenty-seven men were hanged; another which had served in like capacity eleven times, and another, nine.

When he had retired and was traveling about with his own tent show, displaying his awesome ropes, he would lecture and demonstrate just how the rope should be adjusted around a condemned man's neck.

"You got to use good hemp," he would explain, "and stretch it with sandbags until it is an inch thick. I'd not sell one of these ropes for $50."

Someone commented on the size of the hangman's knot.

"Yes, it's extra large," said George, solemnly, "I'll show you why," and he slipped the noose over his own head and pulled the knot up under his left ear.

"See? I place the knot right here, then allow a little slack by draping the rope slightly over the head. Like this. Now, when the body drops, that slight slack and the knot right up under the left ear, the head is jerked slightly to the side, and the neck is snapped instantly." And he would snap his fingers in dramatic fashion.

The people would ask question after question, with George supplying all the answers, while he basked in the glory of his past, unique occupation.

This little man who held the unenviable reputation of having executed several times as many men as any officer in America, was born June 10, 1830, at Landau, Bavaria. The next year, his parents brought him to America, settling in Detroit, Michigan. There he received an education at the city schools. George Maledon was an adventurer, and on reaching the proper age, he left Detroit and headed westward.

Several months later, he found himself in the Choctaw Nation, Indian Territory, where he worked in a lumber mill. Eventually, he came to Fort Smith, Arkansas, and secured a position on the city police force, serving last under Chief Wheeler. When the Civil War broke out, Maledon joined the First Arkansas Federal Battery and served without mishap to the close of hostilities. In 1865, he was appointed a deputy sheriff under Thomas Scott, and later under John H. McClure.

When the United States District Court was moved from Van Buren, Arkansas, to Fort Smith, he served as a deputy United States marshal under Logan S. Roots, acting as turnkey at the prison. A year later, he applied for the job as official court hangman and was accepted. Maledon was holding this position when Judge I. C. Parker arrived. Parker soon

earned the dubious title of "The Hanging Judge," and his hangman, Maledon, was more than willing to carry out his part of the job.

Under his watchful eye, Maledon had things pretty well in order. His uncanny skill with the sixgun, as well as with the ropes, soon spread far and wide. Five men died trying to escape Maledon's jail. Yet, never once did George display any outward sign of excitement or nervousness. He was calm and went about his work undisturbed. However, if anyone mentioned his work to him, he was immediately on the defensive.

Riggs Studio, Fort Smith

George Maledon was the "official" hangman for Judge I. C. Parker, known in terror as "the hanging judge." Maledon became an expert in his "trade," sometimes hanging several in unison.

This is Garrison Street, Fort Smith, Arkansas, in 1880. It appears that a crowd is gathering, perhaps for a hanging.

"It's honest and respectable work, and I aim to do it well," he would retort.

Maledon even tried to keep a rogue's gallery of all the men he had hanged, but his wife disposed of the first batch of tintypes, so he gave it up. He and Judge Parker apparently got along all right. Both men lived on North Thirteenth Street and very often they would be seen walking home together. There is record of only one known disagreement between the hangman and the judge. It seems that Parker wanted several men hanged at night, after a long trial; however, Maledon said that he did his hanging in the daytime only, and would not work at night. Judge Parker apparently considered it a reasonable request, for Maledon won his point.

Although Judge Parker actually sentenced one hundred seventy-two men to die on his gallows, only eighty-eight dropped through the trap doors. The others were either found not guilty after another hearing granted by the United States Supreme Court, or were got-

ten off Scot-free by the noted lawyer, J. Warren Reed, arch enemy of Parker.

Of the eighty-seven men hanged, Maledon asked to be excused from performing the task in only one instance. This was in the case of Sheppard Busby, who, like Maledon, was a former Union soldier. Busby had served as a member of the Fifty-sixth Illinois Regiment during the Civil War, and also was a member of the Grand Army of the Republic. When Busby was sentenced to be hanged, Maledon asked to be excused.

"Why?" asked the surprised Judge Parker, for well he knew how his hangman hesitated to have anyone else ascend his platform in the performance of the gruesome work.

"He's an ex-Union soldier," replied Maledon.

"Oh, all right, you are excused," said Parker, who also was an ex-Union soldier, although only in the home guard.

After Maledon had hanged his first man, a twenty-one-year-old Texan named Daniel H.

112

This is the U.S. jail and courthouse at Fort Smith, Arkansas, where Judge Parker and his hangman built their dubious reputations. Maledon received a total of $8,700 for his services, spread over the years.

Evans, for the murder of a young man named Seabolt, one of the spectators expressed amazement at the short time in which the man had died — two minutes.

"When the man's neck is broken, he is unconscious and death is instant or as near instant as death can be. I have broken the neck of every man I hanged. Every one of my hangings has been a scientific job. I have dropped as many as six through at one time, and twice have hanged five at one time, and there was no quiver in the entire sixteen — not even a foot moved."

Maledon's last hanging occurred on July 30, 1896. The last man to die on Parker's gallows was James Casharago, who was hanged for the murder of Z. E. Thatch. The famous gallows was put to the torch by the city fathers after Maledon and J. Warren Reed had asked to

Riggs Studio, Fort Smith

George Maldeon kept his ropes at home and at the ready, well-lubricated for a quick drop. Strangely, he appeared proud of his work. His pay was $100 per hanging.

113

take them around the country for display purposes.

Parker's hangman stated his greatest disappointment in life was when he was unable to hang personally the man who had murdered his daughter, Anne. Maledon followed the trial religiously, anxiously awaiting the time when he could slip the noose around the neck of Frank Carver, the handsome adventurer who had killed his beautiful Anne. But he was to be cheated out of the satisfaction. After two appeals and trials, Carver was sentenced to life imprisonment for his crime.

Anne Maledon was only eighteen years old when she met the handsome Frank Carver of Muskogee. Anne's story is one of the tragedies of our great West. The daughter of the most famous hangman, Anne was shunned by girls her age, and never was asked to attend local parties, or would the boys seek her hand. Her stepmother made life miserable for her as well, so poor Anne did the best she could with her social life. It was about this time that she accepted Carver's friendship. Of course, she was somewhat shocked when she learned that he had been brought to Fort Smith to stand trial for whiskey-peddling to the Indians. It was not long before she discovered too, that he was a heavy drinker and a professional gambler. So for some time, Anne sought the lonely comfort of her room.

Carver was acquitted on the whiskey charge — a common one in those days — but instead of returning to Muskogee, he remained in Fort Smith, to be with Anne Maledon, he told her. Oddly enough, Carver's hold on poor Anne seemed to be getting stronger instead of weaker, even after she discovered he was already married and had two children. Even this failed to dim her love for him. Her aroused family tried to talk some sense into her head, but Anne felt that for the first time in her life, she was important, and she clung to that belief. So strong were her feelings that she even accompanied Carver to Colorado, where they lived for nearly two years as man and wife. Then Carver had the gall to bring Anne to Muskogee in the hope that his wife would divorce him when she saw him with another woman. However, this she flatly refused to do.

Once while Carver was away from Fort Smith, down in Texas on one of his gambling jaunts, pretty Anne Maledon met a man named Frank Walker. He was a fine young fellow and possessed none of the unfavorable characteristics as shown in the make-up of Carver.

Carver learned of Anne's meetings with Walker and became insanely jealous. Anne now realized that she would be better off if Carver were out of her life completely. She told him this, driving his jealous rage to an uncontrollable degree. On the night of March

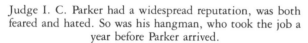
Judge I. C. Parker had a widespread reputation, was both feared and hated. So was his hangman, who took the job a year before Parker arrived.

25, 1895, after drinking heavily, Carver met Anne on the street.

"Anne, darling, I'm going to kill you," he told her.

"What's the matter with you, Frank? You don't kill something you love, as you claim you do me."

"You've been unfaithful to me and must stand the consequences."

Anne saw that the man was mad and meant what he said. She jerked free from his grasp and tried to escape.

"I am sorry to do this, Anne," he said, and shot her four times. Then he turned and ran away as fast as he could, but returned in a few minutes and asked her who had done the shooting.

"You know who shot me, Frank. Why pretend?"

The wounded girl was taken to the hospital, where it was learned she had little chance to survive.

Fort Smith was ablaze with fury at the wanton shooting. People were remarking that they could hardly wait to see the girl's father place the noose around Carver's neck.

Judge Parker issued his famous edict from this high bench of his courtroom: "I sentence you to be hanged by the neck until you are dead . . . dead . . . dead!"

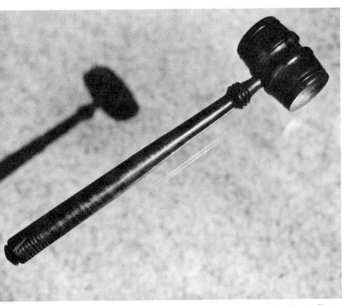

Carl Breihan Collection

This was Judge Parker's gavel, presented him by President U. S. Grant. Like Judge Roy Bean and his "law west of the Pecos," Parker was endeavoring to bring law and order to his region through the courts, and thus tame the raw frontier.

Anne had signed a statement to the effect that Frank Carver had shot her. But Carver's relatives retained the prominent lawyer, J. Warren Reed, to defend the killer, and he began to twist the facts to such an extent that it appeared Carver might escape Maledon's ropes.

The jury found Carver guilty of the murder of Anne Maledon, and Judge Parker sentenced him to be hanged by the neck until he was dead . . . dead . . . dead. . . . Reed, however, took a writ of error to the United States Supreme Court. Parker's decision was reversed and a second trial ordered — a blow to the prestige of Parker's court. On the second go-around, the jury brought in a verdict of guilty with a sentence of life imprisonment.

Those were bitter days for both Maledon and Parker. The hangman had been deprived of sending his daughter's killer through the scaffold trap doors; Parker had been defeated in a verdict by his implacable foe, J. Warren Reed.

Maledon never recovered from the blow. He gave up his job as Parker's official hangman; sold his Fort Smith property, and moved to an eighty-acre farm near Fayetteville, Arkansas. He had even tried the grocery business in Fort Smith in 1894, but he was too close to his beloved Anne and bitter memories.

Farming did not agree with Maledon, so he moved to Tennessee, eventually entering the Veterans Home at Mountain Home, Johnson City, where he died on May 6, 1911 at the age of eighty-one.

Judge Parker died November 17, 1896, two months and seventeen days after his powerful court had been abolished. He was buried in the National Cemetery, Fort Smith, Grave 4000.

Chapter Twelve

Villa's Raiders

IF YOU TOLD someone that a foreign army invaded the United States in 1916, he probably would look at you with a stare of dismay and disbelief. Yet such was the case. It happened when Gen. Pancho Villa crossed the border to raid Columbus, New Mexico. His intent — murder, pillage, and looting.

Pancho Villa? Not the name with which he was born, but the name that ran loud and clear throughout many battles in Mexico, his raids striking terror wherever he went, his loyalty to those who best suited his purpose.

It is known that Francisco "Pancho" Villa was born Doroteo Arango on June 5, 1878, in the state of Durango, Mexico. Not much is known about his parents or if they were legally married. We know the lad remained with his mother, never mentioning his father, no one daring to question him about it in later years.

Born at a time when violence and bloodshed were an everyday occurrence, the young Arango boy became accustomed to that era of brutality, throwing himself into every task with vigor, courage, daring, and recklessness. Unlike millions of peons of the day, the young man decided to make a name for himself, one way or the other. In later years, his men wanted to make him president of Mexico, but he declined, stating he was not the man for the job; that the people needed an educated and compassionate man, not a killer and an outlaw. Besides, he loved his fighting and his women too much to be tied down with matters of state.

Later known only as Pancho Villa, he was in and out of jail numerous times prior to his eighteenth birthday for his open criticism against whatever he did not agree with, especially the ruling body of Mexico at the time.

Finally, he went off on his own, rarely to return home. However, one day word reached him that his mother was looking for him. He hurried to her side.

"Doroteo, your sister Mariana is with child. She will not tell me who the man is."

Pancho talked with his sister. Soon he learned that the man who had made her pregnant was Negrete Lopquez, son of wealthy Don Lopquez. Buckling on his .44 revolver, Pancho leaped upon his mare and dashed off toward the rich man's hacienda.

When he reached his destination, the boy asked to see Negrete. They met in the garden to the rear of the great house.

"What is it? We have nothing in common," sneered Negrete.

"I am Doroteo Arango, brother of Mariana." That is all the boy said before he shot and killed Negrete Lopquez.

This was Pancho's first recorded killing. Now a branded outlaw, with a price on his head, he could do nothing but join up with an outlaw band. He chose that of Juan Parra, a well-known bandit of the region. The following years would bring fame and fortune to the man now called Pancho Villa. He would be called Robin Hood by many, "King of the Mexican Bandits" by others. Yet, his career

117

Arizona Historical Society

Francisco I. Madero was one of the foremost leaders and proclaimed President during the turbulence of the Mexican Revolution. Pancho Villa greatly admired him.

icans, mostly wanted men from Texas and New Mexico.

In February of 1913, Victoriano Huerta was placed in command of the government forces to suppress the insurrection led by Felix Diaz. However, he deserted the cause of President Madero and after forcing the latter's resignation and imprisonment, proclaimed himself provisional president. Huerta captured Pancho Villa at one encounter, but the wily outlaw managed to escape to the United States, where he opened a butcher shop. It is said he did quite well, never paying for any of the cattle he butchered and sold.

When Huerta took over the reigns of government in Mexico, it was not long before Madero was murdered, and the United States refused to recognize the new government.

Things were too peaceful for Pancho Villa back in the United States, so he returned to Mexico to build up his forces. Villa's famed Dordados were well-organized. Each man owned two horses and was issued a 7-mm Mauser rifle and a pair of Colts, with sufficient ammunition for each weapon. Every man wore an olive drab uniform and a Stetson hat.

Villa returned to Mexico in 1914, aiding General Alvaro Obregon and Venustiano Carranza in overthrowing Huerta from the office of president, with Carranza becoming the new leader of Mexico. The border raids of Pancho Villa embroiled Carranza with the United States. In April 1920, a revolution drove him from the capitol. He was slain later in his own camp. Alvaro Obregon took over the government from Carranza in 1920. He effected far-reaching reforms in education, labor, and agrarian fields, and gained recognition of his regime from the United States government in 1923. He left office in 1924 and was re-elected in 1928, but was assassinated on the eve of taking office.

Pancho Villa had no favor with the regime of Carranza, and they offered a reward for him, dead or alive. On March 9, 1916, Villa and his men, six hundred strong or more, invaded Columbus, New Mexico, seeking revenge, it is said, for the non-delivery of war supplies which had been paid for in advance. Why Villa

shows that always he was kind to the poor and down-trodden, and when fighting for what he thought was right, did so with every sinew and muscle of his energy-filled body.

Abandoning a career of cattle rustling and other crimes, Pancho Villa joined Francisco I. Madero late in 1910 in an attempt to unseat Porfirio Diaz from the presidency. Madero had proclaimed himself provisional president of Mexico, and Villa assisted his cause by recruiting arms and ammunition from Texas. Soon Villa was promoted to the rank of colonel of his outfit, which included Mexicans and Amer-

turned against Carranza has never really been determined, although this is what happened.

En route to Columbus, Villa killed two Americans on a ranch near Palomas, Mexico. One of these men, Henry McKinney, was buried in the cemetery at Columbus.

The Mexican invasion began at 2:30 A.M. when Villa and his men crossed the international border into New Mexico. The raid upon Columbus began at 4:25 A.M. on Thursday, March 9, 1916. The Mexicans had taken up positions along the old grade road just west of the station and the cavalry headquarters, while another party was in the street before the Hoover House, it being on the main street in town. The United States Thirteenth Cavalry under Col. Herbert J. Slocum was taken completely by surprise, although word had been sent to Columbus that Villa was operating close by.

The Mexicans crossed the international boundry just west of the gate where troops were always stationed and had partially surrounded the town before the outposts and sentinels were alarmed. In a few minutes following the killing of two of the sentries, the

Venustiano Carranza was another tough revolutionary leader in the Mexican upheaval.

Victoriano Huerta was placed in command of government forces to suppress the insurrection led by Felix Diaz. He once captured Pancho Villa, but the slippery leader escaped.

Mexicans were in every part of the town and camp. It was a complete surprise. From the direction of the Hoover House, the Mexicans advanced in force, shooting as they came. From the west, the raiders in the shelter of the old grade embankment poured a heavy fire into the camp with machine guns and a one-pound rapid-fire gun. The Mexicans advancing from the east found no opposition; they entered the stores they found. They gathered in front of the Commercial Hotel and ordered everyone out of the building. The proprietor and such of his guests who could not escape the back way, gathered at the top of the entrance steps. The men in the party were ordered to advance. They were shot down as soon as they reached the street, and the hotel was set on fire. With the hotel went five other smaller buildings near and in the heart of town.

In a matter of minutes, the American soldiers had advanced and the Mexicans at the

119

These spurs now owned by R. R. Riss II of New York, saw plenty of action on the heels of Pancho Villa.

shelter of the old grade were ousted. The soldiers began to engage the Mexicans, as well as those who had entered town from the east. Disorganized, the soldiers had to fight for their lives before they could secure their equipment, from which they had been separated by roving bands of the raiders. There were no guns and ammunition in the quarters, and the machine guns were cut off by the Mexicans. The soldiers, however, made a break under fire for their equipment, and owing to good fortune, secured it without serious loss.

The first machine gun brought into action beside the railroad track jammed, and it was there that the machine gun troop lost its men. The Mexicans retreated up and over the hill to the west, where their horses were picketed on the parade grounds. The first light of day was just breaking, and the soldiers saw Villa's men forming. They opened up with machine guns and rifles at six hundred yards, and the tangle of dead horses, equipment, and dead and dying men, testified to the deadly aim of the Americans.

The Mexicans began a rapid, though orderly retreat, throwing out a rear guard. From there on, the fight was a running one, with Maj. Frank Tompkins with two troops following the raiders closely. The trail to the border two miles hence was marked by dead horses, piles of equipment and loot taken from the stores which the raiders had packed on horses.

The Mexicans got the surprise of their lives when Lt. Benson, who was stationed at the international gate with a troop, took them on the flank. The lieutenant heard the firing and guessing its cause, deployed his men as skirmishers along the border. He held his fire until the Mexicans were almost on him when his men poured in a deadly fire. Eighteen dead were counted at that point. Of course, Villa's men carried off as many of their wounded as they could. There were four encounters with the raiders after crossing the international line, and the dead Mexicans were found heaped up after every one of them. The Mexicans rode rapidly south, fighting a rear guard action, until they came to some flat country, where they deployed in force. Maj. Frank Tompkins saw the folly of following them farther, and he drew off to a defensive position on high ground. Shortly thereafter, the Americans returned to their camp.

At the time the fight opened, there were parts of four troops and the machine gun platoon in camp. Two of the troops under Major Lindsley were in camp at Moore's ranch on the line four miles from Columbus. These two troops were not engaged, in fact, they did not know of the fight until met by a party of volunteers from Deming, some thirty miles from Columbus. The volunteers had been sent south shortly after daylight by Colonel Slocum. The officer of the day was the only commissioned man in camp, the other officers having cottages in and about Columbus with their families. The officers joined their commands as rapidly as possible. The men of the Thirteenth knew it would be hand-to-hand combat at times, and went into keen action after the first sight of blood. They believed Villa intended that every man, woman, and child in the village should be killed, the bank and stores looted, the soldiers massacred, and all equipment taken into Mexico. But the wily Mexican bandit-raider got away with only a small part of his program, and his losses no doubt made him consider if it were worth the effort.

Pancho Villa retreated toward the Boca Grande River and mountains southeast of the border. This was wild, wooded, and well-watered country, and it would be a difficult task to dislodge him from his retreat.

As Major Tompkins was returning from following the raiders, he was stopped at the international gate by Carranza troops. They said the Americans had no right in Mexico, and they denied that the Carranza garrison at Palomas, four miles south of the border, had anything to do with the raid. However, the major managed to smooth things over and continued on his way.

The quartermaster wagons were busy hauling loads of dead outside the camp and town where a great funeral pyre was kindled. About forty Mexicans were cremated in this fire. The mesquite outside town, and to and across the border was still strewn with Mexican dead and wounded. Luckily, none of the Americans was killed or seriously wounded after the first fight in the camp and town. The Mexican raiders' marksmanship was very poor; had it been otherwise, Villa might have accomplished his mission completely.

The raiders killed J. J. Moore in his home about a mile outside of Columbus and wounded his wife in the leg. They also killed Mrs. M. James, whose house was a short distance from town, and also wounded her husband, who managed to escape.

Bravery and courage were shown to a great degree by Mrs. G. E. Parks, the telephone operator, whose office was near the Hoover House where the fight began. The walls of the little wooden shack were no match for the Mauser bullets which tore through them, nor was there any protection from the flying glass of shattered windows. Yet Mrs. Parks stood by her duty, her child clasped to her breast. She summoned aid and continued to give information to Deming until the danger had passed. She worked in the dark, so her little wooden shack did not attract any of the looters as they raced through Columbus.

After the battle, it was determined that fifteen Americans had been killed and nine wounded, and an educated guess of some one hundred Mexicans slain. Many were the bitter comments in Columbus for the government,

Gen. Alvaro Obregon was another key leader in Mexico.

Andres Garcia   Gen. Alvaro Obregon.

3054
W. H. Horne Co.
(Copyrighted)
El Paso, Tex.

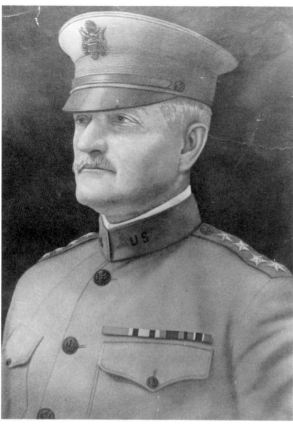

Gen. John J. Pershing, who later gained fame and a place in history heading the American expeditionary forces in World War I, was in charge of troops pursuing Poncho Villa across the border.

failing in its duty to protect American life and property in and out of the United States. That Mexicans should dare to attack a garrisoned town with the intent of wholesale massacre reflected the contempt with which the various Mexican factions viewed the American government. Many people commented also on the fact that the border was practically defenseless, when nearly a thousand men could make a clean getaway over it. The newspapers were critical for the safety of many isolated ranchers and farmers whose property was near the border.

From later information, it was determined that Pancho Villa apparently intended to begin the battle just as the Golden Gate Limited pulled into Columbus. The loot from such a train would have supplied him with much-needed cash. However, his men mistook a train of loaded coal cars that was running special just ahead of the limited train, firing on it and giving ample warning for the limited to remain at Deming until the fighting ceased.

Ten of the Mexican prisoners were taken to Deming by Sheriff Simpson on the following Wednesday. Two were released, two of the men died, and two were operated on and hospitalized. The surving four were arraigned immediately before Judge C. C. Rogers, the sick men to be considered later. Alvaro Obregon was held for the federal grand jury, as he carried stolen property on his person, all stamped with the United States mark. Victoriano Loya and Tomas Gardea were held over, to be tried for murder as participants in the Columbus raid.

In the basement, twelve-year-old Jesus Pius Hes awaited painfully on a cot. The lad was to have his leg amputated at the hip. His wound was badly infected, and the general opinion was that he would not survive the operation. The lad stated that he had attended school in Chihauhua, and that he had lived with his father there. Immediately before the battle, his father left him with the horses just outside Columbus, with instructions that he stay clear of the fighting. Father and son had planned to escape from Villa when the battle started, and to enter the United States. The lad stated in Spanish that Villa forced them to accompany him on the raid, and that he never saw his father again.

News from Washington, D.C. indicated that the Mexican government would cooperate with the Americans in an effort to destroy Pancho Villa and his raiders. At 12:10 P.M. on Wednesday, March 15, the American punitive troops crossed the international boundry at Columbus, four thousand or more strong, equipped with artillery and machine guns. Colonel Dodge left Hachita with three thousand more troops under his command. Others followed until a total of ten thousand men was in the field in pursuit of Pancho Villa.

The troops under command of Gen. John J. Pershing and Colonel Slocum were intent on avenging the deaths of the Americans at Columbus, yet many shook their heads in puzzlement, wondering how the troops would manage to capture the slippery Villa in his favorite haunts. Many feared that Carranza's troops, posing as allies, would not continue the search very long. However sincere the de facto government may be, it was asserted, the irregular troops would not long endure the violation of Mexican territory. The dislike was mutual, racial, and of long standing.

Pancho Villa was last heard of in the Galcana district, making for the foothills of the great Sierra Madres. Airplanes were used to scour the countryside in an effort to locate the fleeing outlaws.

Shortly after midnight on March 15, Colonel Slocum and General Pershing held a conference with Colonel Davila of the Mexican garrison at Palomas. The Mexican officer said he had orders to cooperate with the American forces. When the American troops reached Palomas, they found the village completely deserted. Reports reached the town that many of its male inhabitants had gone to join Villa's brigands.

But Villa was a good leader and also a dreamer. He had delved back into fiction for the use of his name of Pancho Villa, it being the name of a legendary bandit, whose name is still whispered about the country even to this day. He named his favorite stallion Seven Leagues, no doubt after the story of the Seven League Boots. No one really knows how long Carranza's men actually put their heart into the search for Villa; at any rate, General Pershing's pursuit of the bandit lasted one whole year, and at the end of that time, Pancho was still at large. The American forces were withdrawn from Mexico, the hunt for Pancho Villa an utter failure. The troops had not even caught a glimpse of the daring bandit.

In 1920, Pancho Villa was offered amnesty by the Mexican government of that time, and he accepted. He retired in Parral where he bought a large ranch with the gold the government had awarded him for "services rendered." He also bought the ownership of the Parral Bank. Villa had come a long way, indeed. Villa signed a contract with the Mexican government, stating he would not get involved in politics or go on any more raiding rampages or support any political figure whatsoever.

Things went well for several years. Pancho Villa and his men had retired to his immense holdings, where they tilled the soil, built roads, and probably for the first time in their lives did honest work.

On Friday, July 20, 1923, Villa left Parral for his ranch, driving his Dodge touring car. With him went three of his bodyguards. On

"The caissons go rolling along . . ." A U.S. Army wagon train is crossing the Rio Grande, about 1916. Pancho Villa was blamed for much of the border trouble and raids on U.S. towns. He was often described as "a Mexican bandit" and not a hero.

Arizona Historical Society

Gen. Villa, as he fell across
his car door, when killed.

Arizona Historical Society

Pancho Villa died from an assassin's bullet in Parral, Mexico, falling across the door of his open car. The year was 1923. Villa had "retired" to a nearby farm in 1920. What appears to be a lucky shot by a photographer, soon after the killing, may have been pre-arranged as evidence to prove to Villa followers that he was dead.

the outskirts of town, near a small bridge, was a man standing beside the road. The man raised his hand in salute and cried out, "Viva Villa!"

Villa turned to give a return salute when a volley of shots rang out from a nearby building. Pancho Villa died with sixteen bullets in his body. With him died his bodyguards.

His career ended as it had begun . . . steeped in violence and blood.

Bibliography

Books:

Anderson, George B., *History of New Mexico*, Pacific State Publisher, New York, N.Y., 1907.

Beebe, Lucuis & Clegg, Charles, *United States West, Saga of Wells Fargo*, E. P. Dutton Company, New York, N.Y., 1949.

Biggers, Don, *Shackelford County Sketches*, Albany News, 1908.

Boggs, Mae H., *My Playhouse Was A Concord Coach*, Howell-North Press, Oakland, Calif., 1942.

Botkin, B. A., *Treasury of Western Folklore*, Crown Publishers, New York, N.Y., 1951.

Bradley, R. T., *Lives of Frank and Jesse James*, J. W. Marsh Company, St. Louis, Mo., 1882.

Breihan, Carl W., *Badmen of the Frontier*, McBride Company, New York, N.Y., 1957.

———. *Bandit Belle*, Superior Publishing Company, Seattle, Wash., 1971.

———. and Ballert, Marion, *Billy the Kid*, Superior Publishing Company, Seattle, Wash., 1970.

———. *The Complete and Authentic Life of Jesse James*, Frederick Fell Inc., New York, N.Y., 1953.

———. *The Day Jesse James Was Killed*, Frederick Fell Inc., New York, N.Y., 1961.

———. *Escapades of Frank and Jesse James*, Frederick Fell Inc., New York, N.Y., 1974.

———. *Killer Legions of Quantrill*, Superior Publishing Company, Seattle, Wash., 1971.

———. *Outlaws of the Old West*, John Long, Ltd., London, England, 1959.

———. *Quantrill and His Guerrillas*, Swallow Publishing Company, Denver, Colo., 1959.

———. *Younger Brothers*, Naylor Company, San Antonio, Tex., 1961.

Bruffey, George A., *Eighty-One Years in the West*, Butte Miner Company, Butte, Mont., 1925.

Buckbee, Edna B., *Pioneer Days of Angel's Camp*, Calaveras, Calif., 1932.

Burns, W. N., *Tombstone*, Page and Company, Gorden City, N.Y., 1927.

Burton, R. F., *City of the Saints*, Long Book Company, 1951.

Bush, I. J., *Gringo Doctor*, The Caxton Printers, Ltd., Caldwell, Idaho, 1939.

Bushwick, Frank H., *Glamorous Days*, Naylor Company, San Antonio, Tex., 1934.

Canton, Frank M., *Frontier Trails*, Houghton Mifflin Company, New York, N.Y., 1930.

Casey, R. J., *The Texas Border*, Bobbs-Merrill Company, Indianapolis, Ind., 1950.

Chapman, A., *The Pony Express*, G. P. Putnam's Sons, New York, N.Y., 1932.

Chapman, B. B., *Founding of Stillwater*, Times Journal Publishers, Oklahoma City, Okla., 1948.

Chisholm, Joe, *Brewery Gulch*, Naylor Company, San Antonio, Texas, 1949.

Clark, O. S., *Clay Allison of the Washita*, Attica, Ind., 1922.

Cleveland, Agnes Morley, *No Life for A Lady*, Houghton Mifflin Company, Boston, Mass., 1941.

Connelly, Wm. E., *Quantrill and the Border Wars*, Torch Press, Cedar Rapids, Iowa, 1910.

Cook, James H., *Fifty Years on the Frontier*, Yale University Press, New Haven, Conn.

Coolidge, Dane, *Fighting Men of the West*, E. P. Duton Company, New York, N.Y., 1932.

Crittenden, H. H., *Crittenden's Memoirs*, G. P. Putnam's Sons, New York, N.Y., 1936.

Crocker, H. S., *Catalogue of Wells Fargo*, H. S. Crocker Company, San Francisco, Calif., 1893.

Croy, Homer, *Jesse James Was My Neighbor*, Duell, Sloan and Pearce, New York, N.Y., 1949.

Cunningham, Eugene, *Famous in the West*, Hicks-Haywood, El Paso, Tex., 1926.

————. *Triggernometry*, Press of the Pioneers, Inc., New York, N.Y., 1934.

Dalton, Emmett, *When the Daltons Rode*, Doubleday, Doran Company, Garden City, N.Y., 1931.

Dimsdale, T. J., *Vigilantes of Montana*, Montana Press, Virginia City, 1866.

Dobie, F. Frank, *Vaquero of the Brush Country*, Southwest Press, Dalles, Tex., 1929.

Dobie, Frank J., *Flavor of Texas*, Dealey and Lowe, Dallas, Tex., 1936.

Douglas, C. L., *Famous Texas Feuds*, Turner Company, Dallas, Tex., 1936.

Edwards, John N., *Noted Guerrillas*, J. W. Marsh Company, St. Louis, Mo., 1880.

Fulton, Maurice, *Lincoln County War*, Robert N. Mullin, editor, University of Arizona Press, Tucson, Ariz., 1968.

Greer, James K., *Grand Prairie*, Tardy Publishing Company, Dallas, Tex., 1935.

Gillett, James B., *Six Years with the Texas Ranger*, Boeckmann-Jones, Austin, Tex., 1921.

Haley, J. Evetts, *Jeff Milton*, University of Oklahoma Press, Norman, Okla., 1940.

Hanes, Bailey C., *Bill Doolin*, University of Oklahoma Press, Norman, Okla., 1968.

Harlow, Alvin F., *Old Waybills*, Appleton-Century, New York, N.Y., 1934.

Hendricks, George D., *Bad Man of the West*, Naylor Company, San Antonio, Tex., 1941.

Hoole, W. Stanley, *The James Boys Rode South*, Tuscaloosa, Ala., 1955.

House, Boyce, *Cowtown Columnist*, Naylor Company, San Antonio, Tex., 1946.

Hubbs, Barney, *Shadows Along the Pecos*, Pecos, Tex.

Hunter, J. Marvin & Rose, Noah H., *Album of Gunfighters*, Bandera, Tex., 1951.

Huntington, George, *Robber and Hero*, Christian Way Company, Northfield, Minn., 1895.

Jennings, N. A., *A Texas Ranger*, Southwest Press, Dallas, Tex., 1930.

Jensen, Ann, *Texas Ranger's Diary and Scrapbook*, Kaleidograph Press, Dallas, Tex., 1936.

Jones, W. F., *Experiences of a United States Marshal in Oklahoma Territory*, Tulsa, Okla., 1937.

Keleher, Wm. A., *Fabulous Frontier*, Rydal Press, Sante Fe, N.M., 1945.

Kelly, Charles, *Outlaw Trail*, Salt Lake City, Utah, 1938.

King, Frank M., *Mavericks*, Trail's End Publishing Company, Pasadena, Calif., 1947.

Martin, Jack, *Border Boss, John Hughes*, Naylor Company, San Antonio, Tex., 1942.

Nix, E. D., *Oklahombres*, Eden Publishing Company, St. Louis, Mo., 1929.

Otero, Miguel, *My Nine Years as Governor of the Territory of New Mexico*, University of New Mexico, Albuquerque, N.M., 1940.

Pinkerton, Wm. A., *Train Robberies*, International Association Chiefs of Police, Jamestown, Va., 1907.

Poe, Sophie, *Buckboard Days*, Caxton Publishers, Caldwell, Idaho, 1931.

Preece, Harold, *The Dalton Gang*, Hastings House, New York, N.Y., 1963.

Raine, Wm. MacLeod & Barnes, Will C., *Cattle*, Doubleday, Doran Company, Garden City, N.Y., 1930.

Ripley, Thomas, *They Died with Their Boots On*, Doubleday, Doran Company, Garden City, N.Y., 1935.

Robinson, Wm., H., *Story of Arizona*, Berryhill Company, Phoenix, Ariz., 1919.

Rye, Edgar, *The Quirt and the Spur*, W. B. Conkey Company, Chicago, Ill., 1909.

Shipman, O. L. (Mrs.), *Taming the Big Bend*, Marfa, Tex., 1926.

Siringo, Charles A., *A Lone Star Cowboy*, Santa Fe, N.M., 1919.

————. *Riata and Spurs*, Houghton Mifflin Company, New York, N.Y., 1927.

Sonnichsen, C. L., *I'll Die Before I Run*, Harper and Brothers, New York, N.Y., 1951.

Stanley, Fr., *The Grant That Maxwell Bought*, World Press, Denver, Colo., 1952.

————. *Desperadoes of New Mexico*, World Press, Denver, Colo., 1953.

————. *The Cimarron Story*, World Press, Denver, Colo., 1949.

————. *Fort Union*, World Press, Denver, Colo., 1953.

————. *Clay Allison*, World Press, Denver, Colo., 1956.

————. *No Tears for Black Jack Ketchum*, World Press, Denver, Colo., 1958.

Taylor, Drew K., *Taylor's Thrilling Tales of Texas*, Guaranty Bond Printing, San Antonio, Tex., 1926.

Walton, Wm. M., *Life of Ben Thompson,* Edwards and Church, Austin, Tex., 1884.

Webb, Walter P., *The Texas Rangers,* Houghton Mifflin, New York, N.Y., 1935.

Wells, Polk, *Polk Wells,* G. A. Warnica Publishers, Hall, Mo.

Wilson, Neill C., *Treasure Express, Epic Days of the Wells Fargo,* McMillan Company, New York, N.Y., 1936.

White, O. P., *Autobiography of A Durable Sinner,* G. P. Putnam's Sons, New York, N.Y., 1942.

————. *Lead and Likker,* Minton, Balch and Company, New York, N.Y., 1932.

White, Owen, *Them Was the Days,* Minton, Balch and Company, New York, N.Y., 1925.

————. *Out of the Desert,* McMath Company Publishers, El Paso, Tex., 1923.

WPA Project, *Arizona,* Hastings House, New York, N.Y., 1940.

————. *California,* Hastings House, New York, N.Y., 1939.

————. *Colorado,* Hastings House, New York, N.Y., 1941.

————. *Montana,* Hastings House, New York, N.Y., 1940.

————. *New Mexico,* Hastings House, New York, N.Y., 1940.

————. *Texas,* Hastings House, New York, N.Y., 1940.

————. *Wyoming,* Hastings House, New York, N.Y., 1940.

Newspapers and Miscellaneous Periodicals:

Austin *Daily Statesman,* March 12, 1884, forward issues.

Colfax County Court Records, 1887, forward.

Correspondence, Mrs. James Riseley, daughter of Burton Mossman.

Correspondence, Bill Selman, grandson of John Selman.

Cimarron *News & Press,* New Mexico, all related issues.

Canadian *Record,* Texas, all related issues.

California State Historical Society files.

California Department of Correction.

Clayton *Enterprise,* New Mexico, May 7, 1901, forward.

Desert News, August, 1973.

Deming *Graphic,* New Mexico, March, 1916.

Files and Recollections of E. M. Dickey, Man of the Frontier.

Files of Historian Kerry Ross Boren, Salt Lake City, Utah.

Galveston *Daily News,* March 11, 1884, forward.

Great Guns Magazine, March, 1955.

History of Nogales, Arizona-Mexico archives.

History of Lampasas County, History of Texas, state archives.

Hemphill County Court Records, 1887, forward.

Files and Recollections of Robert N. Mullin, noted western historian.

Louisville *Courier-Journal,* all related issues.

Montana State Historical Society archives.

National Archives, Mexico City.

National Archives, Washington, D.C., Depts., Interior-Justice.

National Archives, Washington, D.C., census records.

New Mexico *Historical Review,* April, 1948.

New York Library & Historical Society.

Personal contact and correspondence with members of the James-Younger families, 25 years.

Personal correspondence with Jay Doolin Meek, son of Bill Doolin.

Personal contact and interviews with Buffalo Vernon Averill.

Pioneer West Magazine, October, 1967.

Raton *Daily Range,* New Mexico, all related issues.

Notes of Sam Ream, historian, Dover, Ohio Historical Society.

Porfirio Diaz, Mexican files, Mexico City.

Pony Express files, St. Joseph, Mo.

San Antonio *Daily Express,* March 12, 1884, forward.

San Antonio *Light,* March 14, 1954.

Real West Magazine, April, 1973, Nov., 1967.

Salt Lake *Tribune,* August, 1973.

Southwesterner, June, 1964, Selman and Mullin.

St. Joseph *Gazette,* 1882, forward.

St. Louis *Democrat,* April, 1882, forward.

Santa Fe *New Mexican,* 1879, forward.

Sentinel, Crystal City, Tex., Nov., 1959.

Texas State Historical Society.

The West Magazine, October, 1967.

Wells Fargo History Room, San Francisco, Calif.

Westerners Brand Books, July, 1960, June, 1964, March, 1961, Stacy Osgood.

West of the Pecos Museum, Pecos, Texas, Barney Hubbs.

Twenty-five and more years of personal interviews and travel through thirty-seven states by the author.

Correspondence and personal interviews with Milt Hinkle, whose father was sheriff of Ford County during these hectic days.

Records of Kerry Ross Boren, noted historian of Utah history, and an expert on the lives of the Butch Cassidy bunch.